# man cave QUILTS

LEISURE ARTS, INC.
Little Rock, Arkansas

**EDITORIAL STAFF**

Vice President of Editoral: Susan White Sullivan
Special Projects Director: Susan Frantz Wiles
Director of E-Commerce: Mark Hawkins
Art Publications Director: Rhonda Shelby
Technical Editor: Lisa Lancaster
Technical Writer: Frances Huddleston
Technical Associate: Jean Lewis
Editorial Writer: Susan McManus Johnson
Art Category Manager: Lora Puls
Graphic Artists: Amy Temple, Jacob Casleton,
Stacy Owens, and Becca Snider
Imaging Technician: Stephanie Johnson
Prepress Technician: Janie Marie Wright
Photography Manager: Katherine Laughlin
Contributing Photographer: Mark Mathews
Contributing Photo Stylist: Christy Myers
Manager of E-Commerce: Robert Young

**BUSINESS STAFF**

President and Chief Executive Officer: Rick Barton
Vice President of Sales: Mike Behar
Vice President of Finance: Laticia Mull Dittrich
Director of Corporate Planning: Anne Martin
National Sales Director: Martha Adams
Creative Services: Chaska Lucas
Information Technology Director: Hermine Linz
Controller: Francis Caple
Vice President of Operations: Jim Dittrich
Retail Customer Service Manager: Stan Raynor
Vice President of Purchasing: Fred F. Pruss

Library of Congress Control Number: 2012932913

ISBN-13: 978-1-4647-0480-2

# TABLE OF CONTENTS

## TREAT YOUR SPORTS FAN OR OUTDOORSMAN

to a generous lap throw that also makes a large wall hanging for his favorite retreat. Among these masculine designs you'll find the quilt he would choose for himself! There are themes to please the hunter or fisherman; the football, hockey, or speedway fan; and the nature or maritime enthusiast. He will be amazed that you created a quilt just for him. But you'll know how much fun you had while relaxing with piecing and appliqué!

# MEET
# ROCHELLE
# MARTIN

Rochelle Martin has been quilting and designing for more than 20 years, yet her affection for quilts goes all the way back to her childhood.

She says, "I grew up in a Mennonite community where quilt-making was an important part of life. My mother took me to the local quilting bees, where I learned about the creativity of working with fabric and thread. I sewed my own clothes at an early age, and never forgot the way that quilt-making brought everyone together.

"When I was grown, married, and had children, I began quilting for something to do. Soon, it was a practical decision as I made quilt tops for a store that sold finished comforters filled with wool batting to tourists. After that, I worked in a quilt shop where part of my job was designing patterns to showcase the store's fabric. I enjoyed designing so much, I decided to start my own pattern business.

"Along the way, I noticed there was a lack of designs offered for men's quilts, and I decided to help fill that gap. While designing Sea Journey (see page 64), the idea came to me to create several masculine quilts instead of just one. Eventually, I had patterns in a wide choice of themes so that quilters could make gifts fitting the interests of the men in their lives."

Many of Rochelle's quilt designs have appeared in books and popular quilting magazines. She is also a freelance pattern designer for Clothworks textile company. Recently, she co-authored a book with daughter Laura Day. *Strangled by Flying Geese* is the first book in the Quilted Cat Mystery series, and it offers Rochelle's quilt patterns based on Laura's story.

Rochelle lives in Michigan with her husband and is the owner of Cottage Quilt Designs. Her fun patterns can be found at quilt shops and at her online store, CottageQuiltDesigns.info. She has been a member of the Bay Heritage Quilt Guild in her area and has won ribbons and awards at the guild's quilt shows.

# AT THE RACES

*Quilted by Doreen Clink.*

**Finished Quilt Size:** $56^1/2$" x $67^3/4$"
(144 cm x 172 cm)
**Finished Block Size:** 8" x 8" (20" x 20")

## Fabric Requirements

*Yardage is based on 43"/44" (109 cm/112 cm) wide fabric.*

- $1^1/4$ yds (1.1 m) of green tonal*
- $3/4$ yd (69 cm) of race car print
- $7/8$ yd (80 cm) of blue print
- $1^1/2$ yds (1.4 m) of white print
- $3/4$ yd (69 cm) of black tonal
- 10" x 10" (25 cm x 25 cm) piece of brown tonal
- 8" x 8" (20 cm x 20 cm) piece of red tonal
- 8" x 8" (20 cm x 20 cm) piece of orange print
- 8" x 14" (20 cm x 36 cm) piece of yellow tonal
- $4^1/4$ yds (3.9 m) of fabric for backing
- $1/2$ yd (46 cm) of fabric for binding

*You will also need:*

- 65" x 76" (165 cm x 193 cm) piece of batting
- Paper-backed fusible web
- Embroidery floss to match orange print appliqué

*Print used in quilt shown is a gradation print. If using a gradation print, you will need $1^1/2$ yds (1.4 m).

## Cutting the Pieces

*Follow **Rotary Cutting**, page 86, to cut fabric.*
*Cut all strips from the selvage-to-selvage width. All measurements include $1/4$" seam allowances.*
From green tonal: (***Note:*** *If using a gradation print, follow **Cutting Diagram**, page 7, and use **side setting triangle** pattern, page 13.*)

- Cut 5 **middle border strips B** $2^1/2$" wide.
- Cut 1 strip $12^5/8$" wide. From this strip, cut 3 squares $12^5/8$" x $12^5/8$". Cut squares *twice* diagonally to make 12 **side setting triangles**. (You will use 10 and have 2 left over.)
- Cut 1 strip $6^5/8$" wide. From this strip, cut 2 squares $6^5/8$" x $6^5/8$". Cut squares *once* diagonally to make 4 **corner setting triangles**.
- Cut 1 strip $2^1/2$" wide. From this strip, cut 6 **wide rectangles** $2^1/2$" x $6^1/2$".
- Cut 2 strips $1^1/2$" wide. From these strips, cut 6 **long rectangles** $1^1/2$" x $8^1/2$".

From race car print:

- Cut 5 **middle border strips A** $4^1/2$" wide.

From blue print:

- Cut 7 **outer border strips** 3" wide.
- Cut 1 strip $6^1/2$" wide. From this strip, cut 1 **medium square** $6^1/2$" x $6^1/2$".

*From remainder of strip,*

- Cut 6 **small squares** $5^3/8$" x $5^3/8$".

*Continued on page 7.*

*Continued from page 4.*

**From white print:**
- Cut 5 **inner border strips** 3" wide.
- Cut 4 **wide strips** $2^{1}/_2$" wide.
- Cut 2 **narrow strips** 2" wide.
- Cut 1 strip 7" wide. From this strip, cut 1 **large square** 7" x 7".
  *From remainder of strip,*
  - Cut 6 **small squares** $5^{3}/_8$" x $5^{3}/_8$".
- Cut 2 strips 5" wide. From these strips, cut 12 **very small squares** 5" x 5".

**From black tonal:**
- Cut 4 **wide strips** $2^{1}/_2$" wide.
- Cut 2 **narrow strips** 2" wide.
- Cut 1 **very large square** $7^{1}/_2$" x $7^{1}/_2$".
- Cut 1 **large square** 7" x 7".

**From brown tonal:**
- Cut 6 **long rectangles** $1^{1}/_2$" x $8^{1}/_2$".

**From red tonal:**
- Cut 1 **medium square** $6^{1}/_2$" x $6^{1}/_2$".

**From orange print:**
- Cut 3 **short rectangles** $1^{3}/_8$" x $6^{1}/_2$".

**From yellow tonal:**
- Cut 1 **medium square** $6^{1}/_2$" x $6^{1}/_2$".
- Cut 4 **short rectangles** $1^{3}/_8$" x $6^{1}/_2$".

**From fabric for binding:**
- Cut 7 **binding strips** 2" wide.

### Cutting the Appliqué
*Follow **Preparing Fusible Appliqués**, page 88, and use pattern, page 13, to cut appliqué.*

**From orange print:**
- Cut 1 **circle**.

### Making the Pinwheel Blocks
*Follow **Piecing**, page 87, and **Pressing**, page 88, to make quilt top.*

1. Draw a diagonal line on wrong side of each white **small square**.
2. Matching right sides, place 1 white **small square** on top of 1 blue **small square**. Stitch $1/_4$" from each side of drawn line (**Fig. 1**). Cut along drawn line and press seam allowances to darker fabric to make 2 **Triangle-Squares**. Make 12 Triangle-Squares.

**Fig. 1**

**Triangle-Square** (make 12)

**Cutting Diagram**

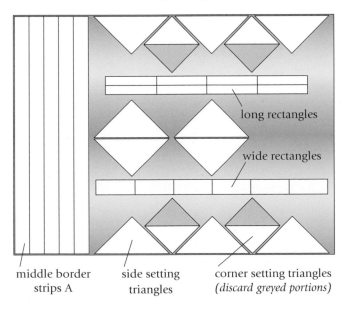

long rectangles

wide rectangles

middle border strips A     side setting triangles     corner setting triangles *(discard greyed portions)*

3. Draw a diagonal line (perpendicular to seam) on wrong side of each **Triangle-Square**.

4. Matching right sides, place 1 **Triangle-Square** on top of 1 white **very small square**. Stitch $1/4$" from each side of drawn line (**Fig. 2**). Cut along drawn line and press seam allowances to larger triangle to make 2 **Unit 1's**. Trim Unit 1 to $4^1/2$" x $4^1/2$". Make 24 Unit 1's.

**Fig. 2**

**Unit 1** (make 24)

5. Sew 2 **Unit 1's** together to make **Unit 2**. Make 12 Unit 2's.

**Unit 2** (make 12)

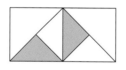

6. Sew 2 **Unit 2's** together to make **Pinwheel Block**. Make 6 **Pinwheel Blocks**.

**Pinwheel Block** (make 6)

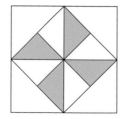

## Making the Flag Blocks

1. Center and fuse **circle** appliqué on black **very large square**. Using 2 strands of embroidery floss, Blanket Stitch (page 94) around circle to make **Unit 3**. Centering circle, trim Unit 3 to $6^1/2$" x $6^1/2$"; set aside.

**Unit 3**

2. Alternating colors, sew 4 yellow **short rectangles** and 3 orange **short rectangles** together to make **Unit 4**. Press seam allowances in 1 direction. Trim Unit 4 to $6^1/2$" x $6^1/2$"; set aside.

**Unit 4**

3. Draw a diagonal line on wrong side of white **large square**.

4. Matching right sides, place white **large square** on top of black **large square**. Stitch ¹/₄" from each side of drawn line (**Fig. 3**). Cut along drawn line and press seam allowances to darker fabric to make 2 **Triangle-Squares**. Discard 1 Triangle-Square. Trim remaining Triangle-Square to 6¹/₂" x 6¹/₂"; set aside.

**Fig. 3**

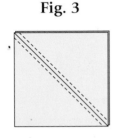

**Triangle-Square**

5. Sew 1 green **long rectangle** and 1 brown **long rectangle** together to make **Unit 5**. Make 6 Unit 5's.

**Unit 5** (make 6)

6. Sew 1 green **wide rectangle** to each of **Unit 3**, **Unit 4**, **Triangle-Square**, and yellow, blue, and red **medium squares** to make 6 **Unit 6's**.

**Unit 6** (make 6)

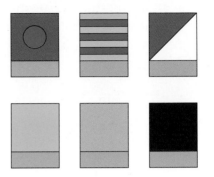

7. Sew 1 **Unit 5** to each **Unit 6** to make 6 **Flag Blocks**.

**Flag Blocks** (make 6)

## Making the Checkered Blocks

1. Sew 2 white **wide strips** and 2 black **wide strips** together to make **Strip Set A**. Press seam allowances to black strips. Make 2 Strip Set A's. Cut across Strip Set A's at 2$\frac{1}{2}$" intervals to make 24 **Unit 7's**.

**Strip Set A** (make 2)     **Unit 7** (make 24)

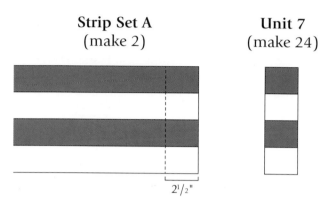

2$\frac{1}{2}$"

2. Sew 4 **Unit 7's** together to make **Large Checkered Block**. Make 6 Large Checkered Blocks.

**Large Checkered Block** (make 6)

3. Sew 2 white **narrow strips** and 2 black **narrow strips** together to make **Strip Set B**. Press seam allowances to black strips. Cut across Strip Set B at 2" intervals to make 16 **Unit 8's**.

**Strip Set B**     **Unit 8** (make 16)

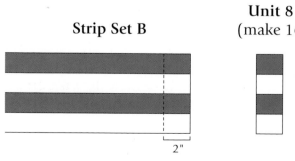

2"

4. Sew 4 **Unit 8's** together to make **Small Checkered Block**. Make 4 Small Checkered Blocks.

**Small Checkered Block** (make 4)

## Assembling the Quilt Top Center

1. Referring to **Assembly Diagram**, sew **Blocks** and **side setting triangles** into *diagonal* **Rows**. Sew **corner setting triangles** to corners to complete quilt top center. Trim edges as needed, leaving $\frac{1}{4}$" seam allowance from points of Blocks.

**Assembly Diagram**

## Adding the Inner Border

*Refer to **Quilt Top Diagram**, page 12, for placement.*

1. Matching ends, cut 1 **inner border strip** in half at fold. Sew 1 half strip and 1 inner border strip together to make **side inner border**. Make 2 side inner borders.
2. Measure *length* across center of quilt top center. Trim side inner borders to determined length. Matching centers and corners, sew side inner borders to quilt top center. Press seam allowances outward.
3. Measure *width* across center of quilt top center (including added borders). Trim remaining inner border strips to determined measurement for **top/bottom inner borders**. Matching centers and corners, sew top/bottom inner borders to quilt top center. Press seam allowances outward.

## Adding the Middle Border

1. Matching ends, cut 1 **middle border strip A** in half at fold. Sew 1 half strip and 1 middle border strip A together to make **side middle border A**. Make 2 side middle border A's.
2. In the same manner, use **middle border strips B** to make 2 **side middle border B's**.
3. Matching long sides, sew 1 side middle border A and 1 side middle border B together to make **side middle border**. Make 2 side middle borders.

### Side Middle Border (make 2)

4. Measure *length* across center of quilt top. Trim side middle borders to determined length. Do not sew borders to quilt top at this time.
5. Matching long sides, sew 1 **middle border strip A** and 1 **middle border strip B** together to make **top middle border**. Repeat to make **bottom middle border**.

6. Measure *width* across center of quilt top. Trim top/bottom middle borders to determined length. Do not sew borders to quilt top at this time.
7. Matching centers and corners, sew side middle borders to quilt top. Press seam allowances outward.
8. Sew 1 **Small Checkered Block** to each end of top/bottom middle borders. Matching centers, seams, and corners, sew top/bottom middle borders to quilt top. Press seam allowances outward.

### Top/Bottom Middle Border (make 2)

## Adding the Outer Border

1. Sew **outer border strips** together, end to end, to make one continuous strip.
2. Measure *length* across center of quilt top. From continuous strip, cut 2 **side outer borders** the determined length. Matching centers and corners, sew side outer borders to quilt top. Press seam allowances outward.
3. Measure *width* across center of quilt top (including added borders). Cut 2 **top/bottom outer borders** the determined length. Matching centers and corners, sew top/bottom inner borders to quilt top. Press seam allowances outward.

## Completing the Quilt

1. Follow **Quilting**, page 89, to mark, layer, and quilt as desired. Quilt shown is machine quilted with an all-over racing pattern which includes race cars, flags, and flames. (See photo of back of quilt, page 13.)
2. Follow **Making a Hanging Sleeve**, page 92, if a hanging sleeve is desired.
3. Use **binding strips** and follow **Binding**, page 92, to bind quilt.

# Quilt Top Diagram

**Back of Quilt**

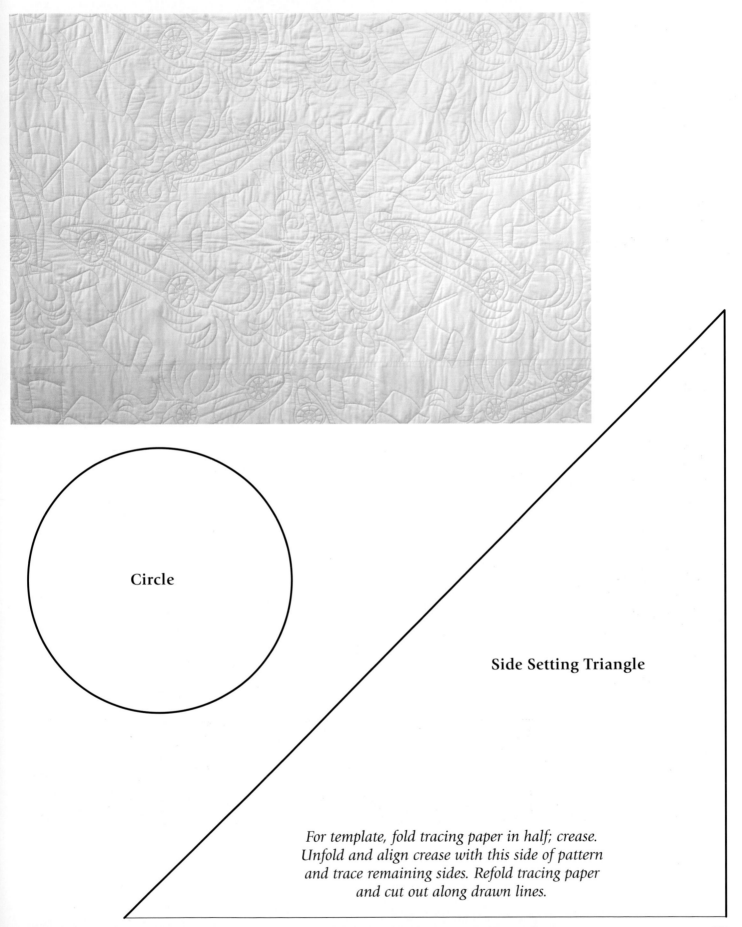

Circle

Side Setting Triangle

*For template, fold tracing paper in half; crease.
Unfold and align crease with this side of pattern
and trace remaining sides. Refold tracing paper
and cut out along drawn lines.*

# Falling Leaves

*Quilted by Doreen Clink.*

**Finished Quilt Size:** 64$^1/_2$" x 76$^1/_2$"
(164 cm x 194 cm)
**Finished Block Size:** 12" x 12" (30 cm x 30 cm)

## Fabric Requirements

*Yardage is based on 43"/44" (109 cm/112 cm) wide fabric.*

1$^3/_4$ yds (1.6 m) of green/gold print
2$^3/_4$ yds (2.5 m) of cream print
1 yd (91 cm) of yellow #1 print*
$^1/_2$ yd (46 cm) of yellow #2 print
$^3/_4$ yd (69 cm) of brown print
$^3/_8$ yd (34 cm) of red #1 print
$^1/_2$ yd (46 cm) of red #2 print
$^1/_4$ yd (23 cm) of orange print
$^1/_4$ yd (23 cm) of yellow-green print
4$^3/_4$ yds (4.3 m) of fabric for backing
$^1/_2$ yd (46 cm) of fabric for binding

*You will also need:*

73" x 85" (185 cm x 216 cm) piece of batting
Paper-backed fusible web
Embroidery floss to match appliqués
(yellow #2 print, brown print, and red #2 print)

*Print used in quilt shown is a diagonal plaid.

## Cutting the Pieces

*Follow **Rotary Cutting**, page 86, to cut fabric. Cut all strips from the selvage-to-selvage width. Large squares are cut larger than needed and will be trimmed after adding appliqués. All measurements include $^1/_4$" seam allowances.*

From green/gold print:
- Cut 7 **outer border strips** 4$^1/_2$" wide.
- Cut 9 **strips** 2$^1/_2$" wide.

From cream print:
- Cut 6 **inner border strips** 2$^1/_2$" wide.
- Cut 4 strips 10$^1/_2$" wide. From these strips, cut 10 **large squares** 10$^1/_2$" x 10$^1/_2$".
- Cut 4 strips 3" wide. From these strips, cut 40 **medium squares** 3" x 3".
- Cut 3 strips 2$^1/_2$" wide. From these strips, cut 40 **small squares** 2$^1/_2$" x 2$^1/_2$".
- Cut 5 strips 2$^1/_2$" wide. From these strips, cut 40 **rectangles** 2$^1/_2$" x 4$^1/_2$".

From yellow #1 print:
- Cut 7 **middle border strips** 2$^1/_2$" wide.
- Cut 5 **strips** 2$^1/_2$" wide.

From yellow #2 print:
- Cut 3 **strips** 2$^1/_2$" wide.

From brown print:
- Cut 6 **strips** 2$^1/_2$" wide.

From red #1 print:
- Cut 4 strips 3" wide. From these strips, cut 40 **medium squares** 3" x 3".

From red #2 print:
- Cut 3 **strips** 2$^1/_2$" wide.

From orange print:
- Cut 3 **strips** 2$^1/_2$" wide.

From yellow-green print:
- Cut 3 **strips** 2$^1/_2$" wide.

From fabric for binding:
- Cut 8 **binding strips** 2" wide.

## Cutting the Appliqués

*Follow **Preparing Fusible Appliqués**, page 88, and use patterns, pages 22-23, to cut appliqués.*

From yellow #2 print:
- Cut 3 **ginkgo leaves**.

From brown print:
- Cut 4 **oak leaves**.

From red #2 print:
- Cut 3 **maple leaves**.

## Making the Leaf Squares

1. Center and fuse 1 ginkgo leaf on 1 large square. Using 2 strands of matching embroidery floss, Blanket Stitch (page 94) around all edges of leaf to make **Ginkgo Leaf Square**. Centering leaf, trim square to $8^1/_2$" x $8^1/_2$". Make 3 Ginkgo Leaf Squares.

**Ginkgo Leaf Square** (make 3)

2. In the same manner, make 4 **Oak Leaf Squares** and 3 **Maple Leaf Squares**.

**Oak Leaf Square** (make 4)

**Maple Leaf Square** (make 3)

## Making the Block A's

*Follow **Piecing**, page 87, and **Pressing**, page 88, to make quilt top.*

1. Sew 4 **strips** (yellow #2, brown, yellow-green, and orange) together to make **Strip Set A**. Press seam allowances in 1 direction. Cut across Strip Set A at $2^1/_2$" intervals to make 10 **Unit 1's**.

Strip Set A

**Unit 1** (make 10)

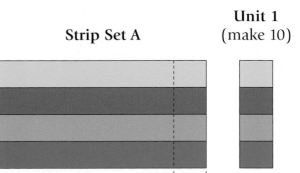

$2^1/_2$"

2. Sew 4 **strips** (red #2, yellow-green, yellow #1, and green/gold) together to make **Strip Set B**. Press seam allowances in 1 direction. Cut across Strip Set B at $2^1/_2$" intervals to make 10 **Unit 2's**.

Strip Set B

**Unit 2** (make 10)

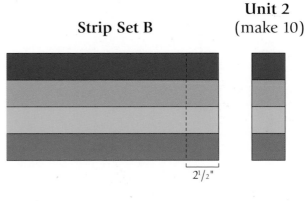

$2^1/_2$"

3. Sew 6 **strips** (yellow #2, brown, orange, yellow #1, red #2, and green/gold) together to make **Strip Set C**. Press seam allowances in 1 direction. Cut across Strip Set C at 2¹/₂" intervals to make 10 **Unit 3's**.

**Strip Set C**

**Unit 3** (make 10)

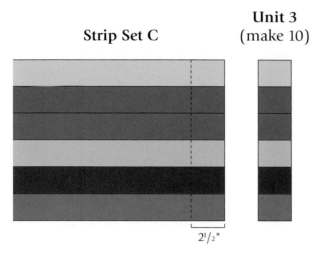

2¹/₂"

4. Sew 6 **strips** (brown, orange, yellow-green, red #2, yellow #2, and green/gold) together to make **Strip Set D**. Press seam allowances in 1 direction. Cut across Strip Set D at 2¹/₂" intervals to make 10 **Unit 4's**.

**Strip Set D**

**Unit 4** (make 10)

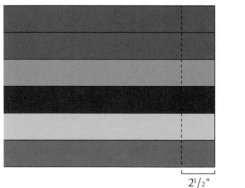

2¹/₂"

5. Sew 1 **Unit 1**, 1 **Unit 2**, and 1 **Leaf Square** together to make **Unit 5**. Make 10 Unit 5's.

**Unit 5** (make 10)

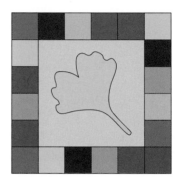

6. Sew 1 **Unit 3**, 1 **Unit 4**, and 1 **Unit 5** together to make **Block A**. Make 10 Block A's.

**Block A** (make 10)

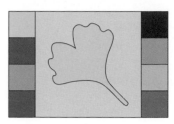

## Making the Block B's

1. Sew 2 **strips** (green/gold and yellow #1) together to make **Strip Set E**. Press seam allowances to darker fabric. Make 3 Strip Set E's. Cut across Strip Set E's at 4¹/₂" intervals to make 20 **Unit 6's**.

**Strip Set E** (make 3)

**Unit 6** (make 20)

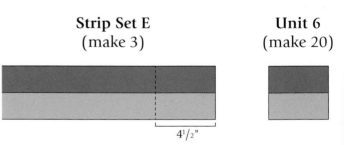

4¹/₂"

2. Sew 2 **strips** (green/gold and brown) together to make **Strip Set F**. Press seam allowances to darker fabric. Make 3 Strip Set F's. Cut across Strip Set F's at 4¹/₂" intervals to make 20 **Unit 7's**.

**Strip Set F**
(make 3)

**Unit 7**
(make 20)

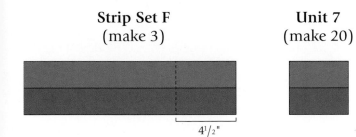

4¹/₂"

3. Sew 1 **Unit 6** and 1 **Unit 7** together to make **Unit 8**. Make 20 Unit 8's.

**Unit 8** (make 20)

4. Sew 2 **Unit 8's** together to make **Unit 9**. Make 10 Unit 9's.

**Unit 9** (make 10)

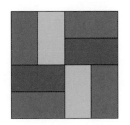

5. Draw a diagonal line on wrong side of each cream **medium square**.

6. Matching right sides, place 1 cream **medium square** on top of 1 red #1 **medium square**. Stitch ¹/₄" from each side of drawn line (**Fig. 1**). Cut along drawn line and press seam allowances to darker fabric to make 2 **Triangle-Squares**. Trim each Triangle-Square to 2¹/₂" x 2¹/₂". Make 80 Triangle-Squares.

**Fig. 1**

**Triangle-Square** (make 80)

7. Sew 2 **Triangle-Squares** and 1 cream **rectangle** together to make **Unit 10**. Make 40 Unit 10's.

**Unit 10** (make 40)

8. Sew 2 cream **small squares** and 1 **Unit 10** together to make **Unit 11**. Make 20 Unit 11's.

**Unit 11** (make 20)

9. Sew 1 **Unit 9** and 2 **Unit 10's** together to make **Unit 12**. Make 10 Unit 12's.

**Unit 12** (make 10)

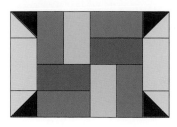

10. Sew 2 **Unit 11's** and 1 **Unit 12** together to make **Block B**. Make 10 Block B's.

**Block B** (make 10)

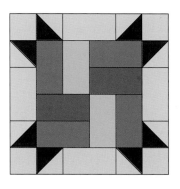

## Assembling the Quilt Top Center
*Refer to **Quilt Top Diagram**, page 21, for block placement and orientation.*
1. Sew 2 **Block A's** and 2 **Block B's** together to make **Row A**. Make 3 Row A's.

**Row A** (make 3)

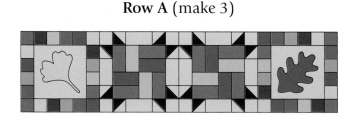

2. Sew 2 **Block A's** and 2 **Block B's** together to make **Row B**. Make 2 Row B's.

**Row B** (make 2)

3. Sew **Rows** together to make quilt top center.

## Adding the Borders
1. Sew **inner border strips** together, end to end, to make one continuous strip.
2. Measure *length* across center of quilt top center. From continuous strip, cut 2 **side inner borders** the determined length. Matching centers and corners, sew side inner borders to quilt top center. Press seam allowances outward.
3. Measure *width* across center of quilt top center (including added borders). Cut 2 **top/bottom inner borders** the determined length. Matching centers and corners, sew top/bottom inner borders to quilt top center. Press seam allowances outward.
4. In the same manner and using **middle border strips** and **outer border strips**, add **middle** and **outer borders**. Press seam allowances outward.

## Completing the Quilt
1. Follow **Quilting**, page 89, to mark, layer, and quilt as desired. Quilt shown is machine quilted. The appliqués are quilted in the ditch. The remainder of the quilt is quilted with an all-over geometrical pattern. (See photo of back of quilt, page 22.)
2. Follow **Making a Hanging Sleeve**, page 92, if a hanging sleeve is desired.
3. Use **binding strips** and follow **Binding**, page 92, to bind quilt.

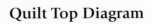

## Quilt Top Diagram

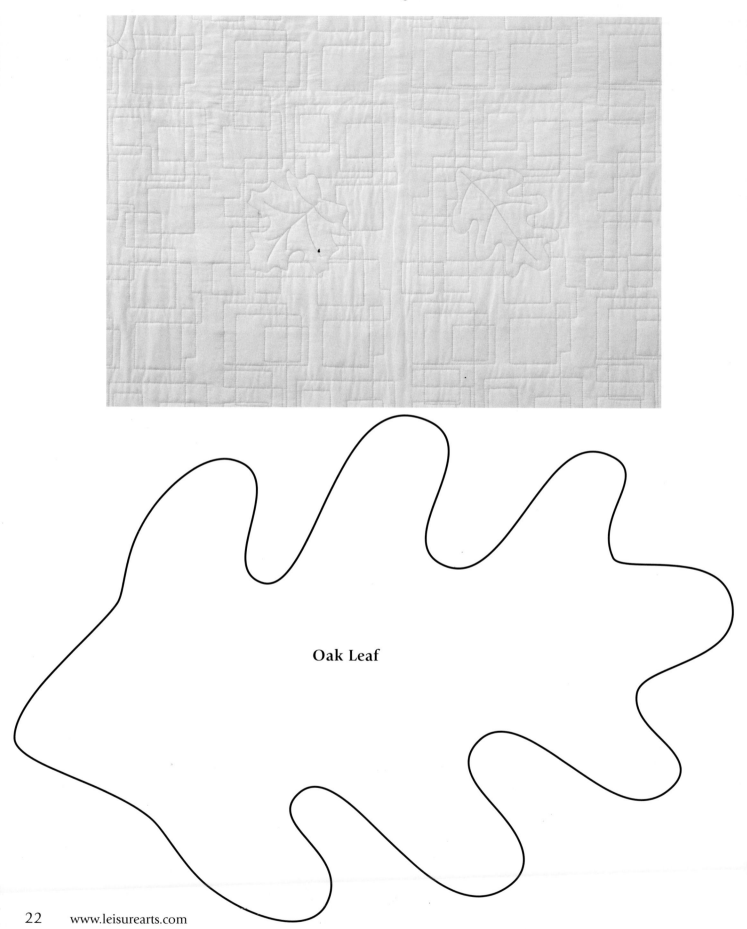

**Oak Leaf**

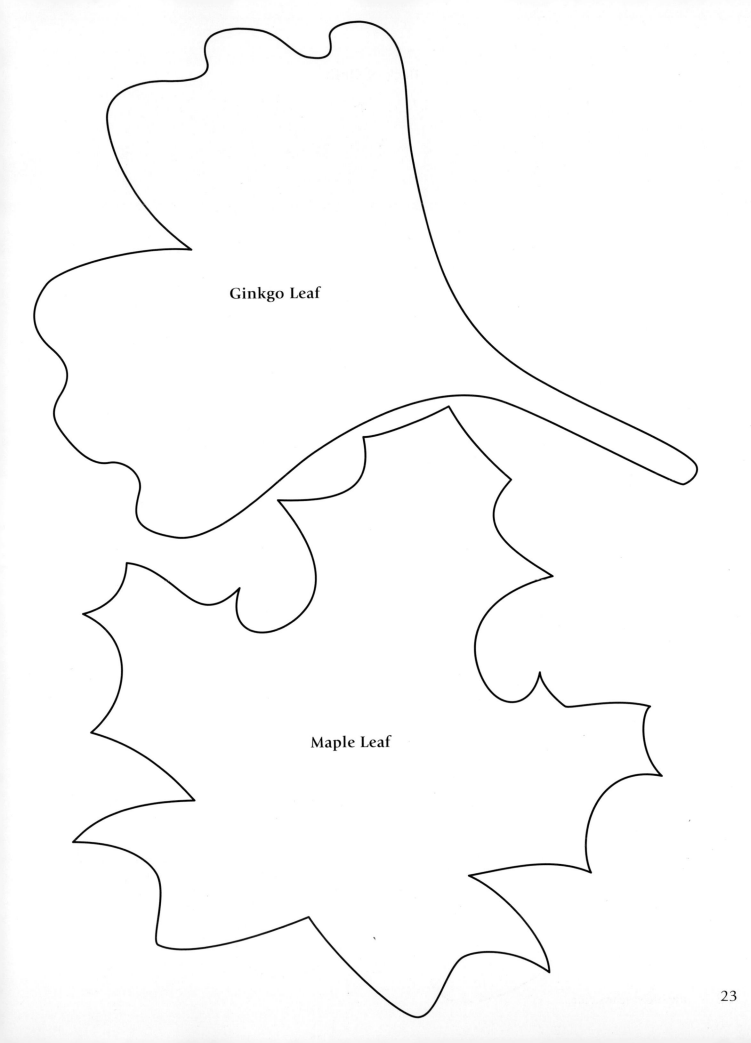

Ginkgo Leaf

Maple Leaf

# Hunting Ground

*Quilted by Doreen Clink.*

**Finished Quilt Size:** 56$^1$/$_2$" x 68$^1$/$_2$"
  (144 cm x 174 cm)
**Finished Hourglass Block Size:** 10" x 10"
  (25 cm x 25 cm)

## Fabric Requirements

*Yardage is based on 43"/44" (109 cm/112 cm) wide fabric. Fat quarters are approximately 21" x 18" (53 cm x 46 cm).*

- 2$^1$/$_2$ yds (2.3 m) of tan batik
- 1$^1$/$_2$ yds (1.4 m) of rust batik
- $^7$/$_8$ yd (80 cm) of black batik
- $^5$/$_8$ yd (57 cm) of dark green batik
- 1 fat quarter of brown tonal
- Scrap of cream tonal
- 6 fat quarters of assorted batiks: tan/blue, gold, brown, orange, light green, and gold/green
- 4$^3$/$_8$ yds (4 m) of fabric for backing
- $^1$/$_2$ yd (46 cm) of fabric for binding

*You will also need:*

- 65" x 77" (165 cm x 196 cm) piece of batting
- Paper-backed fusible web
- Black and cream embroidery floss for appliqués
- Black permanent fabric pen

## Cutting the Pieces

*Follow **Rotary Cutting**, page 86, to cut fabric. Cut all strips from the selvage-to-selvage width. Squares A are cut larger than needed and will be trimmed after adding appliqués. All measurements include $^1$/$_4$" seam allowances.*

**From tan batik:**

- Cut 2 strips 2$^1$/$_2$" wide. From these strips, cut 4 **strips** 2$^1$/$_2$" x 20".
- Cut 2 strips 12$^1$/$_2$" wide. From these strips, cut 4 **squares A** 12$^1$/$_2$" x 12$^1$/$_2$".
- Cut 3 strips 2$^1$/$_2$" wide. From these strips, cut 40 **squares B** 2$^1$/$_2$" x 2$^1$/$_2$".
- Cut 2 strips 2" wide. From these strips, cut 24 **squares C** 2" x 2".
- Cut 1 strip 15$^3$/$_4$". From this strip, cut 2 squares 15$^3$/$_4$" x 15$^3$/$_4$". Cut squares *twice* diagonally to make 8 **side setting triangles**.
- Cut 1 strip 8$^3$/$_8$". From this strip, cut 2 squares 8$^3$/$_8$" x 8$^3$/$_8$". Cut squares *once* diagonally to make 4 **corner setting triangles**.
- Cut 1 strip 3$^3$/$_4$" wide. From this strip, cut 4 **rectangles D** 3$^3$/$_4$" x 6$^1$/$_2$".
- Cut 1 strip 2$^1$/$_2$" wide. From this strip, cut 4 **rectangles E** 2$^1$/$_2$" x 6$^1$/$_2$".
- Cut 2 strips 2" wide. From these strips, cut 8 **rectangles F** 2" x 6$^1$/$_2$".
- Cut 2 strips 2" wide. From these strips, cut 20 **rectangles G** 2" x 2$^1$/$_2$".
- Cut 1 strip 1$^1$/$_2$" wide. From this strip, cut 8 **rectangles H** 1$^1$/$_2$" x 2".

*Continued on page 27.*

*Continued from page 24.*

**From rust batik:**
- Cut 6 **inner border strips** 2¹/₄" wide.
- Cut 2 strips 2¹/₂" wide. From these strips, cut 4 **strips** 2¹/₂" x 20".
- Cut 2 strips 11¹/₄" wide. From these strips, cut 5 squares 11¹/₄" x 11¹/₄". Cut squares *twice* diagonally to make 20 **triangles I**. (You will use 18 and have 2 left over.)
- Cut 1 strip 5¹/₂" wide. From this strip, cut 4 **border squares** 5¹/₂" x 5¹/₂".

**From black batik:**
- Cut 2 strips 2¹/₂" wide. From these strips, cut 4 **strips** 2¹/₂" x 20".
- Cut 2 strips 11¹/₄" wide. From these strips, cut 5 squares 11¹/₄" x 11¹/₄". Cut squares *twice* diagonally to make 20 **triangles J**. (You will use 18 and have 2 left over.)

**From dark green batik:**
- Cut 2 strips 2¹/₂" wide. From these strips, cut 4 **strips** 2¹/₂" x 20".
- Cut 3 strips 2¹/₂" wide. From these strips, cut 20 **rectangles K** 2¹/₂" x 4¹/₂".
- Cut 2 strips 2" wide. From these strips, cut 12 **rectangles L** 2" x 3¹/₂".

**From brown tonal:**
- Cut 2 strips 1¹/₂" x approximately 21". From these strips, cut 10 **rectangles M** 1¹/₂"x 2¹/₂" and 4 **rectangles N** 1¹/₂" x 2".

**From *each* of 6 batik fat quarters:**
- Cut 4 **strips** 2¹/₂" x 20".

**From fabric for binding:**
- Cut 7 **strips** 2" wide.

## Cutting the Appliqués
*Follow **Preparing Fusible Appliqués**, page 88, and use patterns, pages 34-35, to cut appliqués.*

**From brown tonal:**
- Cut 1 **bear** and 1 **bear in reverse**.
- Cut 1 **bear front leg** and 1 **bear front leg in reverse**.
- Cut 1 **bear hind leg** and 1 **bear hind leg in reverse**.
- Cut 1 **deer body** and 1 **deer body in reverse**.
- Cut 1 **deer front leg** and 1 **deer front leg in reverse**.
- Cut 1 **deer hind leg** and 1 **deer hind leg in reverse**.

**From cream tonal:**
- Cut 2 **deer antlers** and 2 **deer antlers in reverse**.

## Making the Appliquéd Blocks
1. Arrange 1 **deer body**, 1 **deer front leg**, 1 **deer hind leg**, 1 **deer antler**, and 1 **deer antler in reverse** in center of 1 **square A**; fuse in place. Using 2 strands of embroidery floss (cream for antlers, black for all other), Blanket Stitch (page 94) around all exposed edges of appliqués to make **Deer Block A**. Use black permanent fabric pen to draw nose and eye. Centering design, trim square to 10¹/₂" x 10¹/₂".

**Deer Block A**

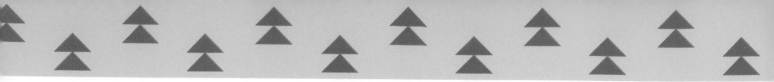

2. In the same manner, make 1 **Deer Block B** using 1 **deer body in reverse**, 1 **deer front leg in reverse**, 1 **deer hind leg in reverse**, 1 **deer antler**, and 1 **deer antler in reverse**.

**Deer Block B**

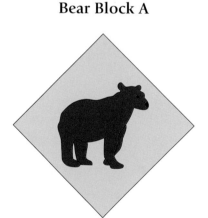

3. In the same manner, make 1 **Bear Block A** using 1 **bear body**, 1 **bear front leg**, and 1 **bear hind leg**.

**Bear Block A**

4. In the same manner, make 1 **Bear Block B** using 1 **bear body in reverse**, 1 **bear front leg in reverse**, and 1 **bear hind leg in reverse**.

**Bear Block B**

## Making the Hourglass Blocks

*Follow **Piecing**, page 87, and **Pressing**, page 88, to make quilt top. Measurements given include seam allowances.*

1. Sew 1 **triangle I** and 1 **triangle J** together to make **Unit 1**. Make 18 Unit 1's.

**Unit 1** (make 18)

2. Sew 2 **Unit 1's** together to make **Hourglass Block**. Hourglass Block should measure $10^1/_2$" x $10^1/_2$". Make 9 Hourglass Blocks.

**Hourglass Block** (make 9)

## Assembling the Quilt Top Center

1. Referring to **Assembly Diagram**, sew **Blocks** and **side setting triangles** into *diagonal* **Rows**.
2. Sew **Rows** together, and then sew **corner setting triangles** to corners to make quilt top center. Trim quilt top center to 43" x 43".

### Assembly Diagram

## Adding the Tree Units

1. Draw a diagonal line on wrong side of each **square B** and **square C**.
2. With right sides together, place 1 **square B** on 1 end of 1 **rectangle K** and stitch along drawn line. Trim $1/4$" from stitching line (**Fig. 1**). Press seam allowances to triangle (**Fig. 2**).

**Fig. 1**          **Fig. 2**

3. Place another **square B** on opposite end of **rectangle K**. Stitch and trim as shown in **Fig. 3**. Press seam allowances to triangle to complete **Flying Geese A**. Flying Geese A should measure $4^1/_2$" x $2^1/_2$". Make 20 Flying Geese A's.

**Fig. 3**

**Flying Geese A** (make 20)

4. In the same manner and using **squares C** and **rectangles L**, make 12 **Flying Geese B's**. Flying Geese B should measure $3^1/_2$" x 2".

**Flying Geese B** (make 12)

5. Sew 2 **rectangles G** and 1 **rectangle M** together to make **Unit 2**. Press seam allowances to rectangle M. Unit 2 should measure $4^1/_2$" x $2^1/_2$". Make 10 Unit 2's.

**Unit 2** (make 10)

6. Sew 2 **rectangles H** and 1 **rectangle N** together to make **Unit 3**. Press seam allowances to rectangle N. Unit 3 should measure $3^1/_2$" x 2". Make 4 Unit 3's.

**Unit 3** (make 4)

7. Sew 2 **Flying Geese A's** and 1 **Unit 2** together to make **Unit 4**. Press seam allowances toward top of "tree." Unit 4 should measure $4^1/2$" x $6^1/2$". Make 10 Unit 4's.

**Unit 4** (make 10)

8. Sew 3 **Flying Geese B's** and 1 **Unit 3** together to make **Unit 5**. Press seam allowances toward top of "tree." Unit 5 should measure $3^1/2$" x $6^1/2$". Make 4 Unit 5's.

**Unit 5** (make 4)

9. Sew 5 **Unit 4's**, 2 **Unit 5's**, 2 **rectangles D**, 2 **rectangles E**, and 4 **rectangles F** together to make **Tree Panel**. Press seam allowances to rectangles. Tree Panel should measure 43" x $6^1/2$". Make 2 Tree Panels.

**Tree Panel** (make 2)

10. Referring to **Quilt Top Diagram**, page 33, sew **Tree Panels** to quilt top center.

## Adding the Inner Border

1. Sew **inner border strips** together, end to end, to make one continuous strip.
2. Measure *length* across center of quilt top center. From continuous strip, cut 2 **side inner borders** the determined length. Matching centers and corners, sew side inner borders to quilt top center. Press seam allowances outward.
3. Measure *width* across center of quilt top center (including added borders). Cut 2 **top/bottom inner borders** the determined length. Matching centers and corners, sew top/bottom inner borders to quilt top center. Press seam allowances outward.

## Adding the Outer Border

1. Sew 5 **strips** (black, tan/blue, rust, dark green, and gold) together to make **Strip Set A**. Press seam allowances in 1 direction. Make 4 Strip Set A's. Cut across Strip Set A's at $5^1/2$" intervals to make 10 **Unit 6's**.

**Strip Set A**
(make 4)

**Unit 6**
(make 10)

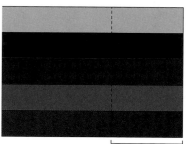

$5^1/2$"

2. Sew 5 **strips** (brown, orange, light green, tan, and gold/green) together to make **Strip Set B**. Press seam allowances in 1 direction. Make 4 Strip Set B's. Cut across Strip Set B's at 5¹/₂" intervals to make 12 **Unit 7's**.

**Strip Set B**
(make 4)

**Unit 7**
(make 12)

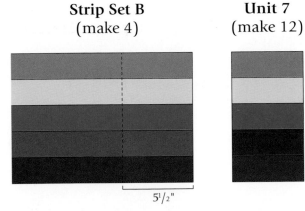

3. Remove the gold/green strip from *each of 2* **Unit 7's** (Fig. 4). Sew 3 **Unit 6's**, 2 **Unit 7's**, and 1 **partial Unit 7** (with strip removed) together to make **side outer border**. Make 2 side outer borders.

**Fig. 4**

4. Remove the tan and gold/green strips from *each of 2* **Unit 7's** (Fig. 5). Sew 2 **Unit 6's**, 2 **Unit 7's**, and 1 **partial Unit 7** (with strips removed) together to make **top outer border**. Repeat to make **bottom outer border**.

**Fig. 5**

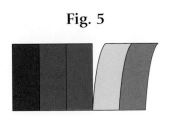

5. Measure *length* across center of quilt top. Measure length of side outer borders. If measurements are not the same, make some of the seams in borders slightly larger or smaller as needed. *Do not* sew side outer borders to quilt top at this time.

6. Measure *width* across center of quilt top. Measure length of top/bottom outer borders. If measurements are not the same, make some of the seams in borders slightly larger or smaller as needed.

7. Matching centers and corners, sew side outer borders to quilt top.

8. Sew 1 **corner square** to each end of top/bottom outer borders. Matching centers and corners, sew side outer borders to quilt top.

## Completing the Quilt

1. To help stabilize the edges and prevent any seams from separating, stay-stitch around the quilt top approximately $1/8$" from the edge.
2. Follow **Quilting**, page 89, to mark, layer, and quilt as desired. Quilt shown is machine quilted. The appliqués are quilted in the ditch. The remainder of the quilt is quilted with an all-over leaf pattern. (See photo of back of quilt.)
3. Follow **Making a Hanging Sleeve**, page 92, if a hanging sleeve is desired.
4. Use **binding strips** and follow **Binding**, page 92, to bind quilt.

**Back of Quilt**

**Quilt Top Diagram**

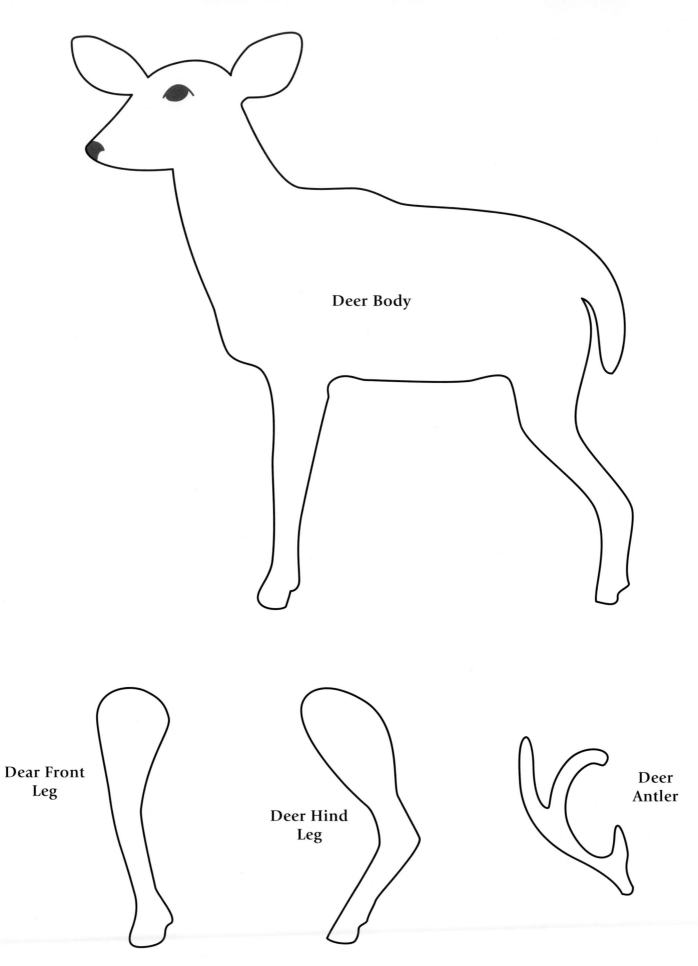

Deer Body

Dear Front
Leg

Deer Hind
Leg

Deer
Antler

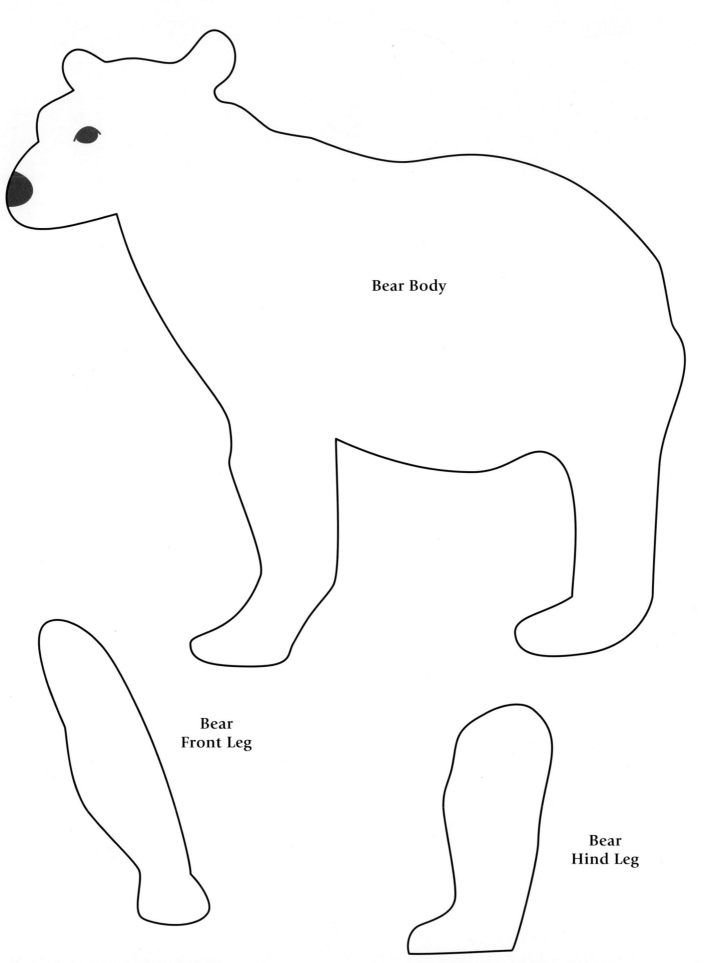

Bear Body

Bear
Front Leg

Bear
Hind Leg

# Morning's Catch

*Quilted by Doreen Clink.*

**Finished Quilt Size:** 48$^1/_2$" x 64$^1/_2$"
(123 cm x 164 cm)
**Finished Block Sizes:** 12" x 12" (30 cm x 30 cm)
and 8" x 16" (20 cm x 41 cm)

## Fabric Requirements

*Yardage is based on 43"/44" (109 cm/112 cm) wide fabric.*

1$^1/_4$ yds (1.1 m) of blue/green batik (outer border and blocks)

1 yd (91 cm) of cream batik (inner border and blocks)

$^1/_2$ yd (46 cm) of brown batik (middle border)

$^1/_4$ yd (23 cm) of grey/brown batik (blocks)

$^3/_8$ yd (34 cm) of dark blue batik (blocks)

$^3/_8$ yd (34 cm) of light blue batik (blocks)

$^3/_8$ yd (34 cm) of medium green batik (blocks)

$^3/_8$ yd (34 cm) of orange batik (blocks)

$^3/_8$ yd (34 cm) of red/brown dotted batik (blocks)

$^1/_4$ yd (23 cm) of grey/tan dotted batik (letters)

$^1/_4$ yd (23 cm) of brown speckled batik (blocks and fish)

$^1/_8$ yd (11 cm) of light grey speckled batik (fish, rod and reel)

$^1/_8$ yd (11 cm) of light green speckled batik (fish)

$^1/_8$ yd (11 cm) of gold speckled batik (fish)

$^1/_8$ yd (11 cm) of black tonal (rod and reel)

Scrap of brown tonal (rod handle)

4$^1/_8$ yds (3.8 m) of fabric for backing

$^1/_2$ yd (46 cm) of fabric for binding

*You will also need:*

57" x 73" (145 cm x 185 cm) piece of batting

Paper-backed fusible web

Black permanent marking pen

Embroidery floss to match appliqués (grey/tan dotted, brown speckled, light grey speckled, light green speckled, gold speckled, black tonal, and brown tonal)

Black #3 pearl cotton

Water-soluble fabric pen

## Cutting the Pieces

*Follow **Rotary Cutting**, page 86, to cut fabric. Cut all strips from the selvage-to-selvage width. Rectangles A and B are cut larger than needed and will be trimmed after adding appliqués. All measurements include $^1/_4$" seam allowances.*

**From blue/green batik:**

- Cut 6 **outer border strips** 4$^1/_2$" wide.
- Cut 1 **strip** 2$^1/_2$" wide.
- Cut 1 **rectangle A** 8$^1/_2$" x 14$^1/_2$".
- Cut 1 **rectangle G** 5$^1/_2$" x 10$^1/_2$".

**From cream batik:**

- Cut 5 **inner border strips** 2$^1/_2$" wide.
- Cut 2 **strips** 8$^1/_2$" wide. From these strips, cut 4 **rectangles A** 8$^1/_2$" x 14$^1/_2$" and 1 **rectangle B** 8$^1/_2$" x 10$^1/_2$".

**From brown batik:**

- Cut 5 **middle border strips** 2$^1/_2$" wide.

**From grey/brown batik:**

- Cut 1 **strip** 2$^1/_2$" wide.
- Cut 1 **rectangle F** 5$^1/_2$" x 6$^1/_2$".

*Continued on page 39.*

*Continued from page 36.*

**From dark blue batik:**
- Cut 2 **strips** 2½" wide.
- Cut 1 **rectangle D** 3½" x 10½".

**From light blue batik:**
- Cut 2 **strips** 2½" wide.
- Cut 1 **rectangle H** 3½" x 16½".

**From medium green batik:**
- Cut 1 **strip** 2½" wide.
- Cut 1 strip 8½" wide. From this strip, cut 1 **rectangle A** 8½" x 14½".
  *From remainder of strip,*
  - Cut 2 **rectangles C** 5½" x 10½".

**From orange batik:**
- Cut 1 **strip** 2½" wide.
- Cut 1 strip 8½" wide. From this strip, cut 1 **rectangle A** 8½" x 14½" and 1 **rectangle E** 8½" x 6½".

**From red/brown dotted batik:**
- Cut 1 **strip** 2½" wide.
- Cut 1 **rectangle A** 8½" x 14½".
- Cut 1 **rectangle D** 3½" x 10½".

**From brown speckled batik:**
- Cut 1 **strip** 2½" wide.

**From fabric for binding:**
- Cut 7 **binding strips** 2" wide.

## Cutting the Appliqués

*Follow **Preparing Fusible Appliqués**, page 88, and use patterns, pages 46-51, to cut appliqués.*

**From grey/tan dotted batik:**
- Cut the **letters B A I T**.
- Cut the **letters B A S S**.
- Cut the **letters T R O U T**.
- Cut the **letters P E R C H**.
- Cut the **letters S A L M O N**.

**From brown speckled batik:**
- Cut 1 **fish body**.
- Cut 1 **fin set**.

**From light grey speckled batik:**
- Cut 1 **fish body**.
- Cut 1 **fin set**.
- Cut 1 **outer reel**.
- Cut 1 **rod highlight**.

**From light green speckled batik:**
- Cut 1 **fish body in reverse**.
- Cut 1 **fin set in reverse**.

**From gold speckled batik:**
- Cut 1 **fish body**.
- Cut 1 **fin set**.

**From black tonal:**
- Cut 1 **rod**.
- Cut 1 **inner reel**.

**From brown tonal:**
- Cut 1 **rod handle**.

## Making the Appliquéd Rectangles

1. Center and fuse **letters B A I T** on cream **rectangle B**. Using 2 strands of matching embroidery floss, Blanket Stitch (page 94) around all edges of appliqués to make **bait rectangle**. Centering word, trim rectangle to 8½" x 6½".

### Bait Rectangle

2. In the same manner, use remaining **letters** and cream **rectangles A** to make **bass rectangle**, **trout rectangle**, **perch rectangle**, and **salmon rectangle**. Centering word, trim each rectangle to 6½" x 12½".

### Word Rectangles

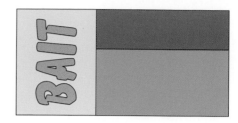

3. Arrange light green speckled **fish body in reverse** and **fin set in reverse** in the center of orange **rectangle A**; fuse in place. Blanket Stitch around all exposed edges of appliqués to make **fish rectangle**. Using black permanent marking pen, draw eye. Centering design, trim rectangle to $6^1/2$" x $12^1/2$".

4. In the same manner, appliqué brown speckled **fish** (body and fin set) onto blue/green **rectangle A**, gold speckled **fish** onto medium green **rectangle A**, and light grey speckled **fish** onto red/brown dotted **rectangle A**. Centering design, trim each rectangle to $6^1/2$" x $12^1/2$".

**Fish Rectangles**

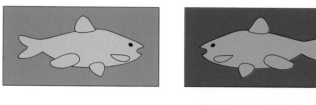

## Making the Large Rectangle Blocks

*Follow **Piecing**, page 87, and **Pressing**, page 88, to make quilt top. Measurements given include seam allowances.*

1. Sew 1 medium green **rectangle C** and dark blue **rectangle D** together to make **Unit 1**.

**Unit 1**

2. Sew **bait rectangle** and **Unit 1** together to make **Bait Block**. Block should measure $8^1/2$" x $16^1/2$".

**Bait Block**

3. Sew grey/brown **rectangle F** and blue/green **rectangle G** together to make **Unit 2**.

**Unit 2**

4. Sew **Unit 2** and light blue **rectangle H** together to make **Block A**. Block should measure $8^1/2$" x $16^1/2$".

**Block A**

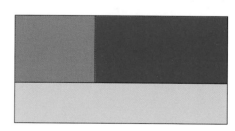

5. Sew medium green **rectangle C** and red/brown dotted **rectangle D** together to make **Unit 3**.

**Unit 3**

6. Sew **Unit 3** and orange **rectangle E** together to make **Block B**. Block should measure $8^1/_2$" x $16^1/_2$".

### Block B

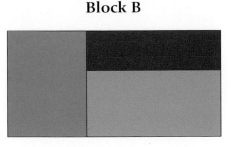

7. Sew light green speckled and orange **fish rectangle** and **bass rectangle** together to make **Bass Block**. Bass Block should measure $12^1/_2$" x $12^1/_2$".

### Bass Block

8. Sew brown speckled and blue/green **fish rectangle** and **trout rectangle** together to make **Trout Block**. Trout Block should measure $12^1/_2$" x $12^1/_2$".

### Trout Block

9. Sew gold speckled and medium green **fish rectangle** and **perch rectangle** together to make **Perch Block**. Perch Block should measure $12^1/_2$" x $12^1/_2$".

### Perch Block

10. Sew light grey speckled and red/brown dotted **fish rectangle** and **salmon rectangle** together to make **Salmon Block**. Salmon Block should measure $12^1/_2$" x $12^1/_2$".

### Salmon Block

## Making the Nine-Patch Blocks

1. Sew 1 medium green **strip** and 1 blue/green **strip** together to make **Strip Set A**. Cut across Strip Set A at 4¹/₂" intervals to make 8 **Unit 4's**.

**Strip Set A**  **Unit 4** (make 8)

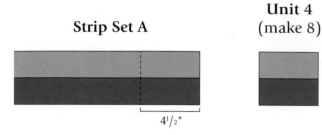

2. Sew 1 dark blue **strip** and 1 light blue **strip** together to make **Strip Set B**. Make 2 Strip Set B's. Cut across Strip Set B's at 4¹/₂" intervals to make 12 **Unit 5's**.

**Strip Set B** (make 2)  **Unit 5** (make 12)

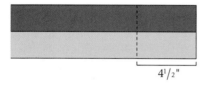

3. Sew 1 brown speckled **strip** and 1 orange **strip** together to make **Strip Set C**. Cut across Strip Set C at 4¹/₂" intervals to make 8 **Unit 6's**.

**Strip Set C**  **Unit 6** (make 8)

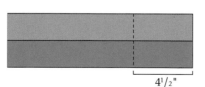

4. Sew 1 red/brown dotted **strip** and 1 grey/brown **strip** together to make **Strip Set D**. Cut across Strip Set D at 4¹/₂" intervals to make 8 **Unit 7's**.

**Strip Set D**  **Unit 7** (make 8)

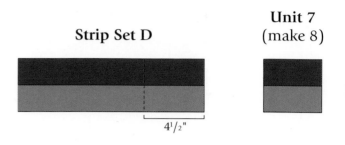

5. Sew 1 **Unit 4**, 1 **Unit 5**, and 1 **Unit 6** together to make **Unit 8**. Make 4 Unit 8's.

**Unit 8** (make 4)

6. Sew 2 **Unit 5's** and 1 **Unit 7** together to make **Unit 9**. Make 4 Unit 9's.

**Unit 9** (make 4)

7. Sew 1 **Unit 7**, 1 **Unit 6**, and 1 **Unit 4** together to make **Unit 10**. Make 4 Unit 10's.

**Unit 10** (make 4)

8. Sew 1 **Unit 8**, 1 **Unit 9**, and 1 **Unit 10** together to make **Nine-Patch Block**. Block should measure 12¹/₂" x 12¹/₂". Make 4 Nine-Patch Blocks.

**Nine-Patch Block** (make 4)

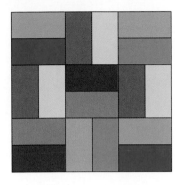

## Assembling the Quilt Top Center

1. Sew **Bait Block**, **Block A**, and **Block B** together to make *vertical* **Row A**.

**Row A**

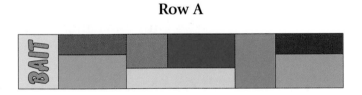

2. Sew 2 **Nine-Patch Blocks**, **Bass Block**, and **Trout Block** together to make *vertical* **Row B**.

**Row B**

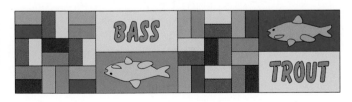

3. Sew 2 **Nine-Patch Blocks**, **Perch Block**, and **Salmon Block** together to make *vertical* **Row C**.

**Row C**

4. Referring to **Quilt Top Diagram**, page 45, sew **Rows** together to make quilt top center.

## Adding the Borders

1. Sew **inner border strips** together, end to end, to make one continuous strip.

2. Measure *length* across center of quilt top center. From continuous strip, cut 2 **side inner borders** the determined length. Matching centers and corners, sew side inner borders to quilt top center. Press seam allowances outward.

3. Measure *width* across center of quilt top center (including added borders). Cut 2 **top/bottom inner borders** the determined length. Matching centers and corners, sew top/bottom inner borders to quilt top center. Press seam allowances outward.

4. In the same manner and using **middle border strips** and **outer border strips**, add **middle** and **outer borders**. Press seam allowances outward.

## Adding the Rod and Reel Appliqués

1. Referring to **Quilt Top Diagram**, arrange and fuse **rod**, **rod highlight**, **rod handle**, **outer reel**, and **inner reel** onto quilt top. Using 2 strands of matching embroidery floss, Blanket Stitch all exposed edges.

2. Using water-soluble pen, draw fishing line and hook. Cut a length of pearl cotton long enough to cover entire line plus about 10". Tuck 1 end of pearl cotton through quilt top at tip of rod. Use 2 strands of black embroidery floss to Couch pearl cotton along drawn line (see **Couching**, page 95).

## Completing the Quilt

1. Follow **Quilting**, page 89, to mark, layer, and quilt as desired. Quilt shown is machine quilted. The appliqués are quilted in the ditch and "scales" are added to the fish. The remainder of the quilt is quilted with an all-over bubble pattern. (See photo of back of quilt.)

2. Follow **Making a Hanging Sleeve**, page 92, if a hanging sleeve is desired.

3. Use **binding strips** and follow **Binding**, page 92, to bind quilt.

**Back of Quilt**

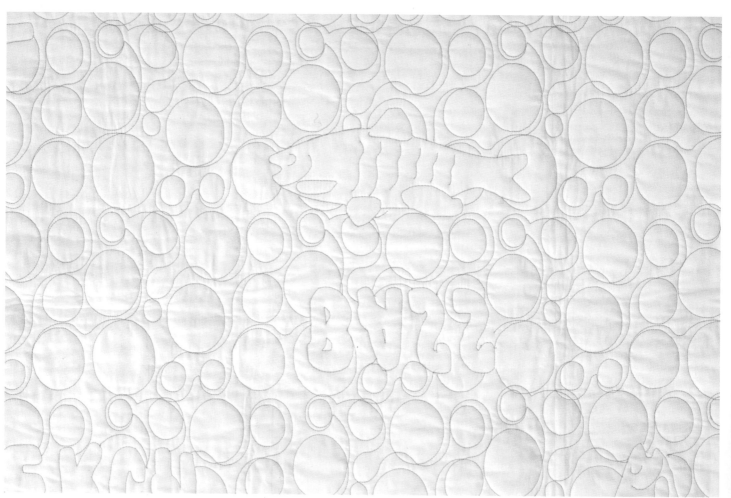

## Quilt Top Diagram

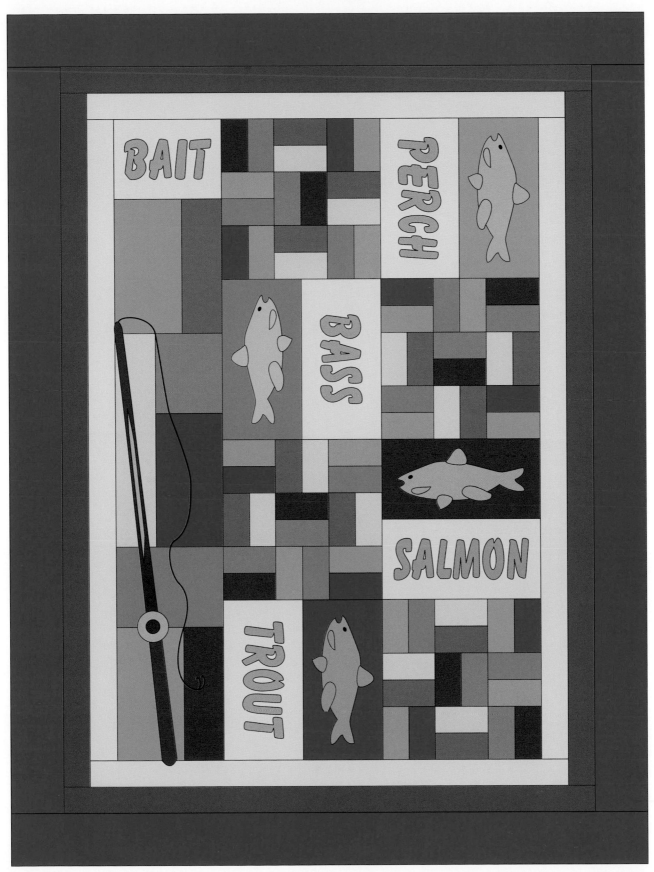

**Fin Set**

**Fish Body**
*Grey area indicates eye. Blue lines
indicate suggested quilting lines.*

www.leisurearts.com

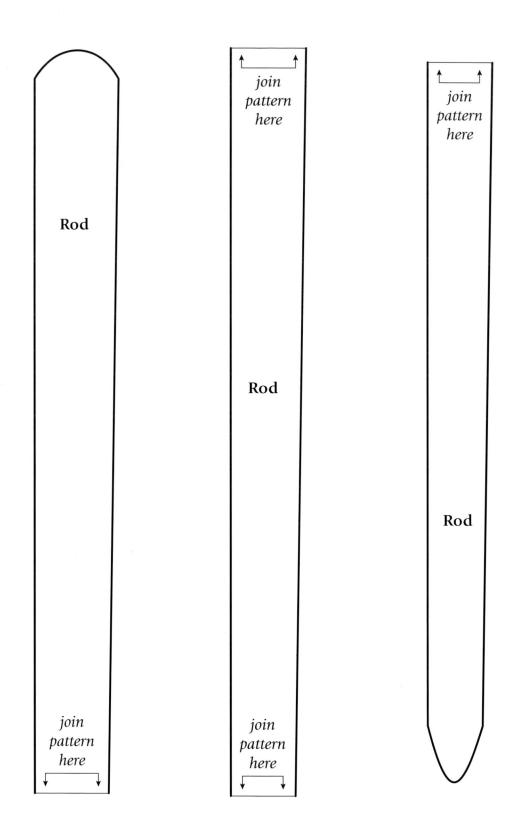

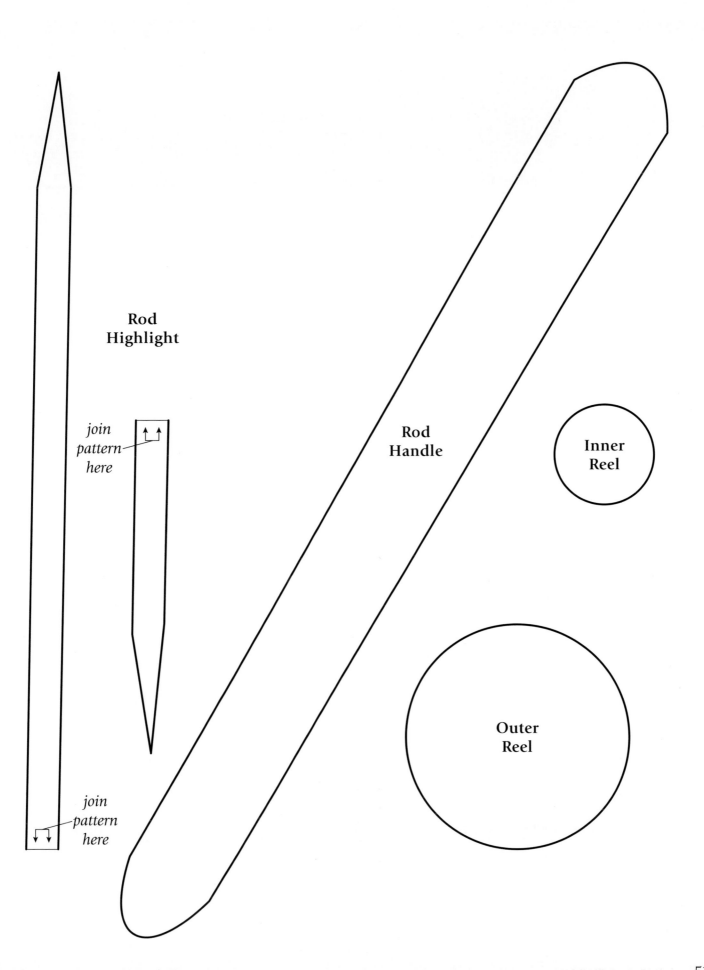

Rod
Highlight

*join
pattern
here*

Rod
Handle

Inner
Reel

*join
pattern
here*

Outer
Reel

# National Pride

*Quilted by Doreen Clink.*

**Finished Quilt Size:** 58¹/₂" x 70¹/₂"
  (149 cm x 179 cm)
**Finished Block Size:** 9" x 9" (23 cm x 23 cm)

## Fabric Requirements
*Yardage is based on 43"/44" (109 cm/112 cm) wide fabric.*

  1⁵/₈ yds (1.5 m) of blue tonal
  1¹/₈ yds (1 m) of red print
  1 yd (91 cm) of tan print
  ⁷/₈ yd (80 cm) of cream tonal
  1¹/₂ yds (1.4 m) of gold print
  ¹/₄ yd (23 cm) of hockey print
  4¹/₂ yds (4.1 m) of fabric for backing
  ¹/₂ yd (46 cm) of fabric for binding
*You will also need:*
  67" x 79" (170 cm x 201 cm) piece of batting
  Paper-backed fusible web
  Embroidery floss to match appliqués (blue
    tonal and hockey print)

## Cutting the Pieces
*Follow **Rotary Cutting**, page 86, to cut fabric. Cut all strips from the selvage-to-selvage width. Large squares are cut larger than needed and will be trimmed after adding appliqués. All measurements include ¹/₄" seam allowances.*

**From blue tonal:**
- Cut 6 **outer border strips** 4¹/₂" wide.
- Cut 2 **strips** 2³/₄" wide.

**From red print:**
- Cut 2 **strips** 2³/₄" wide.
- Cut 1 strip 11¹/₂" wide. From this strip, cut 3 **large squares** 11¹/₂" x 11¹/₂".
- Cut 1 strip 4" wide. From this strip, cut 6 **medium squares** 4" x 4".
- Cut 1 strip 3¹/₂" wide. From this strip, cut 6 **small squares** 3¹/₂" x 3¹/₂".
- Cut 2 strips 3¹/₂" wide. From these strips, cut 6 **large rectangles** 3¹/₂" x 9¹/₂".
- Cut 1 strip 3¹/₂" wide. From this strip, cut 6 **small rectangles** 3¹/₂" x 6¹/₂".

**From tan print:**
- Cut 2 **strips** 2³/₄" wide.
- Cut 1 strip 11¹/₂" wide. From this strip, cut 3 **large squares** 11¹/₂" x 11¹/₂".
- Cut 1 strip 4" wide. From this strip, cut 6 **medium squares** 4" x 4".
- Cut 2 strips 3¹/₂" wide. From these strips, cut 18 **small squares** 3¹/₂" x 3¹/₂".
- Cut 1 strip 2¹/₂" wide. From these strips, cut 12 **very small squares** 2¹/₂" x 2¹/₂".

**From cream tonal:**
- Cut 10 **sashing and inner border strips** 2¹/₂" wide.

**From gold print:**
- Cut 6 **middle border strips** 2¹/₂" wide.
- Cut 2 **strips** 2³/₄" wide.
- Cut 2 strips 11¹/₂" wide. From these strips, cut 6 **large squares** 11¹/₂" x 11¹/₂".
- Cut 1 strip 4¹/₂" wide. From this strip, cut 4 **border squares** 4¹/₂" x 4¹/₂" wide.

**From fabric for binding:**
- Cut 7 **binding strips** 2" wide.

## Cutting the Appliqués

*Follow **Preparing Fusible Appliqués**, page 88, and use patterns, pages 60-63, to cut appliqués.*

From blue tonal:
- Cut 6 **large stars**.
- Cut the **letters H O C K E Y**.

From hockey print:
- Cut 6 **small stars**.

## Making the Appliquéd Blocks

1. Center 1 **large star** and 1 **small star** on 1 gold **large square**; fuse in place. Using 2 strands of matching embroidery floss, Blanket Stitch (page 94) around all edges of large and small stars to make **Star Block**. Centering stars, trim Star Block to $9^1/2$" x $9^1/2$". Make 6 Star Blocks.

**Star Block** (make 6)

2. Center and fuse the **letters H, C, and E** to 3 red **large squares**. Center and fuse the **letters O, K, and Y** to 3 tan **large squares**. Using 2 strands of matching embroidery floss, Blanket Stitch around all edges of letters to make 6 **Letter Blocks**. Centering letters, trim Letter Blocks to $9^1/2$" x $9^1/2$".

**Letter Block** (make 6)

## Making the Four-Patch Blocks

*Follow **Piecing**, page 87, and **Pressing**, page 88, to make quilt top.*

1. Sew 1 blue **strip** and 1 tan **strip** together to make **Strip Set A**. Press seam allowances to the darker fabric. Make 2 Strip Set A's. Cut across Strip Set A's at 5" intervals to make 12 **Unit 1's**.

**Strip Set A** (make 2)    **Unit 1** (make 12)

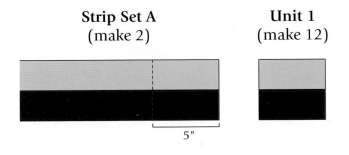

2. Sew 1 red **strip** and 1 gold **strip** together to make **Strip Set B**. Press seam allowances to the darker fabric. Make 2 Strip Set B's. Cut across Strip Set B's at 5" intervals to make 12 **Unit 2's**.

**Strip Set B** (make 2)    **Unit 2** (make 12)

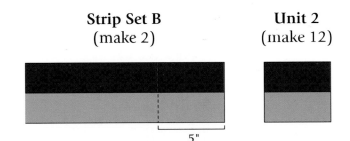

3. Sew 1 **Unit 1** and 1 **Unit 2** together to make **Unit 3**. Make 12 Unit 3's.

**Unit 3** (make 12)

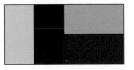

4. Sew 2 **Unit 3's** together to make **Four-Patch Block**. Block should measure 9¹/₂" x 9¹/₂" including seam allowances. Make 6 Four-Patch Blocks.

**Four-Patch Block** (make 6)

## Making the Maple Leaf Blocks

1. Draw a diagonal line on wrong side of each tan **medium square**.
2. Matching right sides, place 1 tan **medium square** on top of 1 red **medium square**. Stitch ¹/₄" from each side of drawn line (**Fig. 1**). Cut along drawn line and press seam allowances to darker fabric to make 2 **Triangle-Squares**. Trim Triangle-Squares to 3¹/₂" x 3¹/₂". Make 12 Triangle-Squares.

**Fig. 1**

**Triangle-Square** (make 12)

3. Draw a diagonal line on wrong side of 12 tan **small squares**.
4. With right sides together, place 1 marked **small square** on 1 end of 1 red **large rectangle** and stitch along drawn line (**Fig. 2**). Trim ¹/₄" from stitching line (**Fig. 3**) and press open to make **Unit 4**. Make 6 Unit 4's.

| **Fig. 2** | **Fig. 3** |
|---|---|

**Unit 4** (make 6)

5. With right sides together, place 1 marked **small square** on 1 end of 1 red **small rectangle** and stitch along drawn line (**Fig. 4**). Trim ¹/₄" from stitching line (**Fig. 5**) and press open to make **Unit 5**. Make 6 Unit 5's.

| **Fig. 4** | **Fig. 5** |
|---|---|

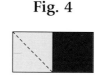

**Unit 5** (make 6)

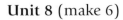

6. Draw a diagonal line on wrong side of each tan **very small square**.
7. With right sides together, place 1 tan **very small square** on 1 corner of 1 red **small square** and stitch along drawn line (**Fig. 6**). Trim ¹/₄" from stitching line (**Fig. 7**) and press open (**Fig. 8**).

**Fig. 6**      **Fig. 7**

**Fig. 8**

8. In the same manner, sew 1 tan **very small square** to the opposite side of red **small square** to make **Unit 6**. Make 6 Unit 6's.

**Unit 6** (make 6)

9. Sew 1 **Unit 5** and 1 **Unit 6** together to make **Unit 7**. Make 6 Unit 7's.

**Unit 7** (make 6)

10. Sew 2 **Triangle-Squares** and 1 tan **small square** together to make **Unit 8**. Make 6 Unit 8's.

**Unit 8** (make 6)

11. Sew 1 **Unit 4**, 1 **Unit 7**, and 1 **Unit 8** together to make **Maple Leaf Block**. Block should measure 9¹/₂" x 9¹/₂" including seam allowances. Make 6 Maple Leaf Blocks.

**Maple Leaf Block** (make 6)

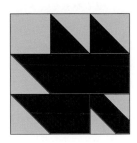

## Assembling the Quilt Top Center

*Refer to **Quilt Top Diagram**, page 59, for placement.*

1. Paying close attention to **Block** placement and orientation, sew 4 Blocks together to make *vertical* **Row**. Row should measure 9¹/₂" x 54¹/₂" including seam allowances. Make 4 Rows.
2. Sew **sashing and inner border strips** together, end to end, to make one continuous strip. From this strip, cut 3 **sashings** 54¹/₂" long. Set remainder of continuous strip aside for inner border.
3. Sew **Rows** and **sashings** together to make quilt top center.

## Adding the Borders

1. Measure *length* across center of quilt top center. From continuous strip, cut 2 **side inner borders** the determined length. Matching centers and corners, sew side inner borders to quilt top center. Press seam allowances outward.
2. Measure *width* across center of quilt top center (including added borders). Cut 2 **top/bottom inner borders** the determined length. Matching centers and corners, sew top/bottom inner borders to quilt top center. Press seam allowances outward.
3. Sew **middle border strips** together, end to end, to make one continuous strip.
4. In the same manner as inner border, add **middle borders**. Press seam allowances outward.
5. Sew **outer border strips** together, end to end, to make one continuous strip.
6. Measure *length* across center of quilt top. From continuous strip, cut 2 **side outer borders** the determined length. Do not sew side outer borders to quilt top at this time.
7. Measure *width* across center of quilt top. From continuous strip, cut 2 **top/bottom outer borders** the determined length. Sew 1 **corner square** to each end of top/bottom borders. Do not sew top/bottom borders to quilt top at this time.
8. Matching centers and corners, sew side and then top and bottom borders to quilt top.

## Completing the Quilt

1. Follow **Quilting**, page 89, to mark, layer, and quilt as desired. Quilt shown is machine quilted. The appliqués are quilted in the ditch and outline quilted. The remainder of the quilt has an all-over star pattern. (See photo of back of quilt.)
2. Follow **Making a Hanging Sleeve**, page 92, if a hanging sleeve is desired.
3. Use **binding strips** and follow **Binding**, page 92, to bind quilt.

**Back of Quilt**

## Quilt Top Diagram

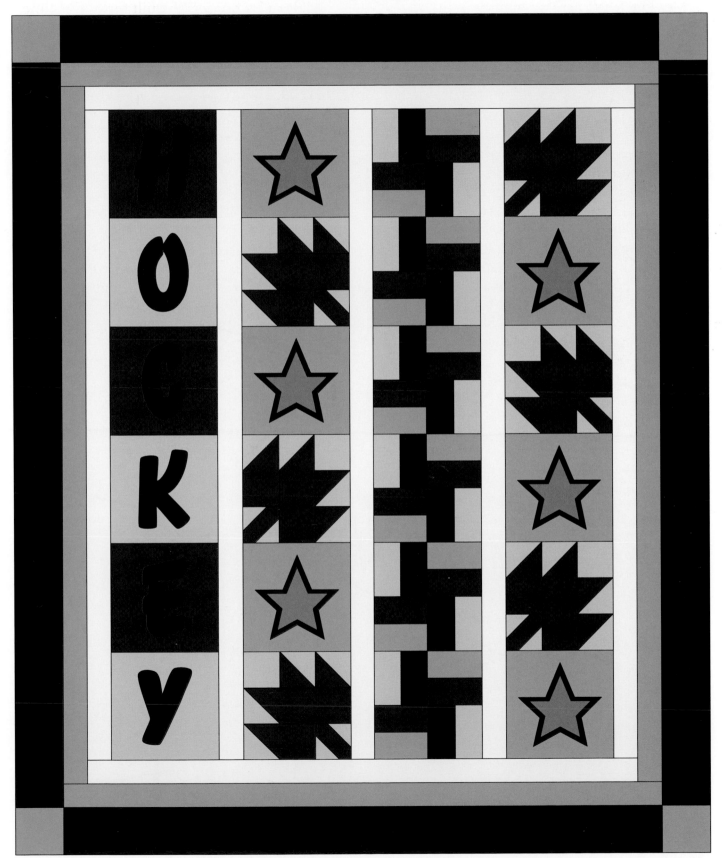

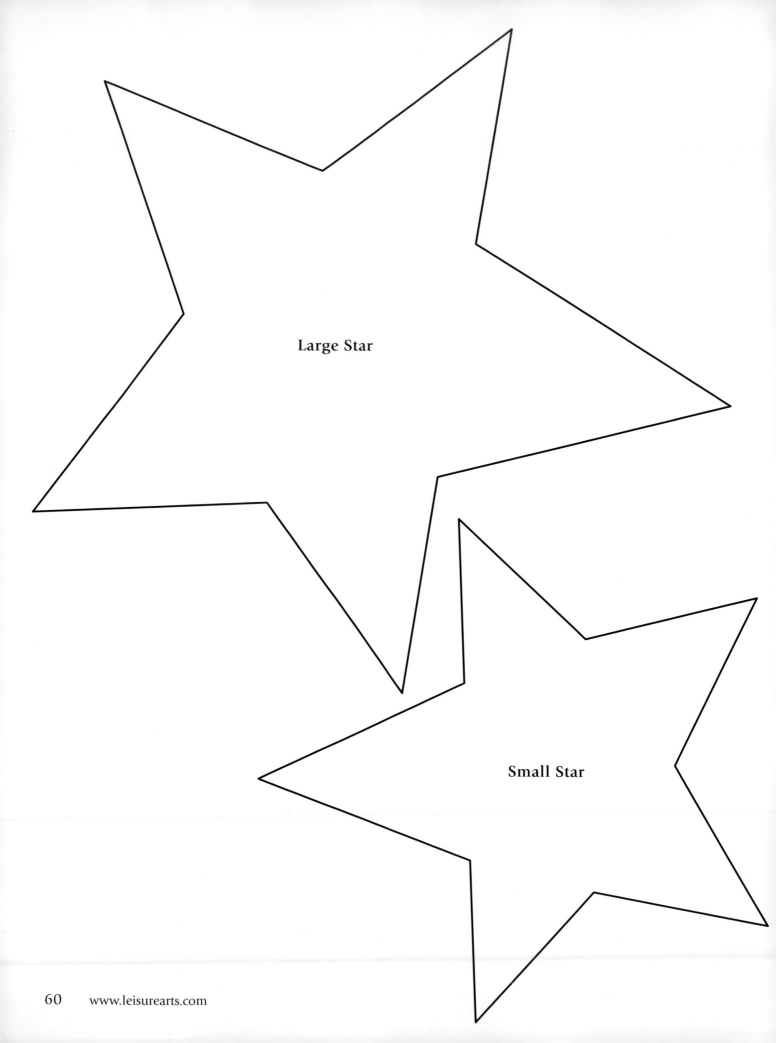

Large Star

Small Star

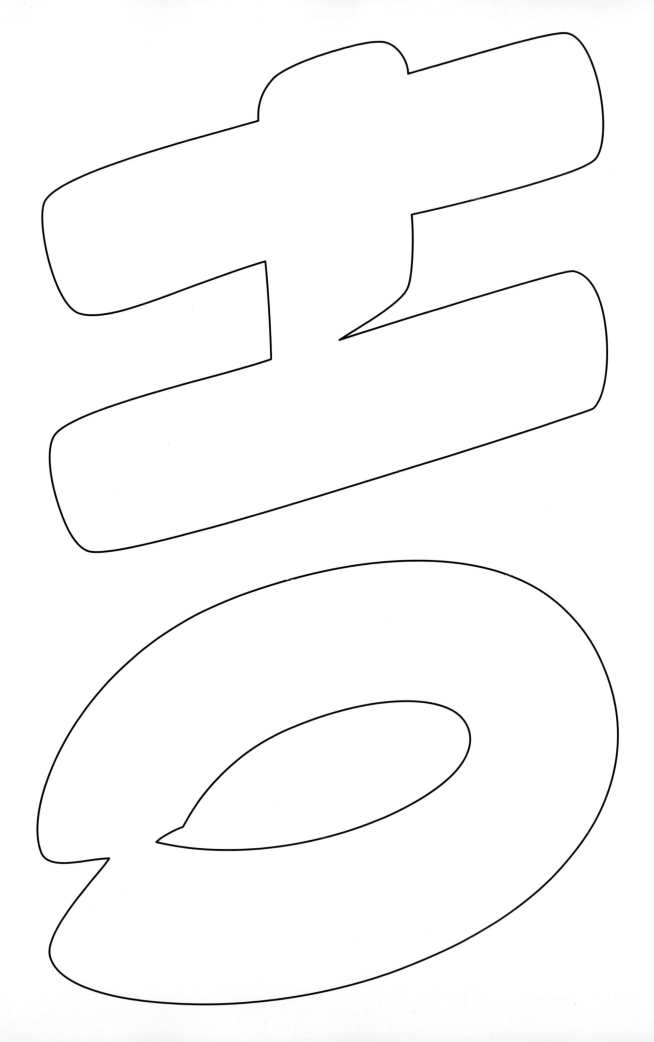

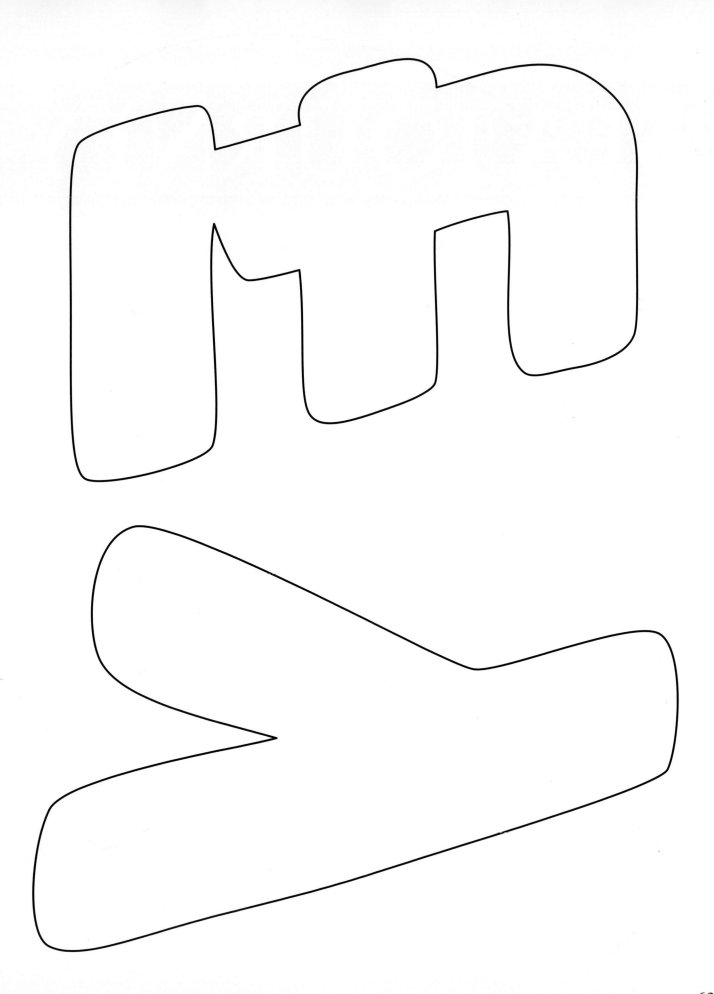

63

# SEA JOURNEY

*Quilted by Carol Rose.*

**Finished Quilt Size:** 60¹/₂" x 72¹/₂"
   (154 cm x 184 cm)
**Finished Block Size:** 6" x 6" (15 cm x 15 cm)

## Fabric Requirements

*Yardage is based on 43"/44" (109 cm/112 cm) wide fabric.*

   3¹/₈ yds (2.9 m) of light blue tonal
   1¹/₄ yds (1.1 m) of medium blue tonal
   ⁷/₈ yd (80 cm) of blue small print
   ⁷/₈ yd (80 cm) of cream tonal
   ³/₄ yd (69 cm) of red tonal
   Scraps of gold tonal and brown tonals
   4¹/₂ yds (4.1 m) of fabric for backing
   ¹/₂ yd (46 cm) of fabric for binding

*You will also need:*

   69" x 81" (175 cm x 206 cm) piece of batting
   Paper-backed fusible web
   Embroidery floss to match appliqués
     (medium blue tonal, blue small print,
     cream tonal, red tonal, gold tonal, and
     brown tonal)

## Cutting the Pieces

*Follow **Rotary Cutting**, page 86, to cut fabric. Cut all strips from the selvage-to-selvage width. Large squares are cut larger than needed and will be trimmed after adding appliqués. All measurements include ¹/₄" seam allowances. **Note:** 1⁹/₁₆" is halfway between 1¹/₂" and 1⁵/₈" on your ruler.*

**From light blue tonal:**

- Cut 4 **wide strips** 2" wide.
- Cut 3 **narrow strips** 1⁹/₁₆" wide.
- Cut 1 strip 8¹/₂" wide. From this strip, cut 4 **large squares** 8¹/₂" x 8¹/₂".
- Cut 4 strips 6¹/₂" wide. From these strips, cut 20 **medium squares** 6¹/₂" x 6¹/₂".
- Cut 4 strips 3¹/₂" wide. From these strips, cut 40 **small squares** 3¹/₂" x 3¹/₂".
- Cut 1 **center square** 12¹/₂" x 12¹/₂".

*From remainder of width,*

- Cut 3 strips 2¹/₂" wide. From these strips, cut 32 squares 2¹/₂" x 2¹/₂". Cut squares *once* diagonally to make 64 **small triangles**.
- Cut 4 strips 4" wide. From these strips, cut 32 squares 4" x 4". Cut squares *once* diagonally to make 64 **large triangles**.
- Cut 2 strips 4³/₈" wide. From these strips, cut 16 squares 4³/₈" x 4³/₈". Cut squares *twice* diagonally to make 64 **medium triangles**.

*Continued on page 67.*

*Continued from page 64.*

From medium blue tonal:

- Cut 3 **narrow strips** $1^9/_{16}$" wide.
- Cut 4 strips 4" wide. From these strips, cut 32 squares 4" x 4". Cut squares *once* diagonally to make 64 **large triangles**.
- Cut 2 strips $4^3/_8$" wide. From these strips, cut 16 squares $4^3/_8$" x $4^3/_8$". Cut squares *twice* diagonally to make 64 **medium triangles**.
- Cut 2 strips $2^1/_2$" wide. From these strips, cut 32 squares $2^1/_2$" x $2^1/_2$". Cut squares *once* diagonally to make 64 **small triangles**.

From blue small print:

- Cut 7 **outer border strips** $3^1/_2$" wide.

From cream tonal:

- Cut 7 **middle border strips** 2" wide.
- Cut 2 **wide strips** 2" wide.

From red tonal:

- Cut 6 **inner border strips** 2" wide.
- Cut 2 **wide strips** 2" wide.

From fabric for binding:

- Cut 8 **binding strips** 2" wide.

## Cutting the Appliqués

*Follow **Preparing Fusible Appliqués**, page 88, and use patterns, pages 74-77, to cut appliqués.*

From medium blue tonal:

- Cut 1 water (**F**).

From blue small print:

- Cut 4 inner compass points (**P**).

From cream tonal:

- Cut 1 of *each* sail (**G-M**).

From red tonal:

- Cut 4 outer compass points (**O**).
- Cut 1 hull (**D**).
- Cut 2 flags (**N**).

From gold tonal:

- Cut 4 compass centers (**Q**).
- Cut 1 hull trim (**E**).

From brown tonal:

- Cut 1 of *each* mast (**A-B**).
- Cut 1 boom (**C**).

## Making the Corner and Chain Blocks

*Follow **Piecing**, page 87, and **Pressing**, page 88, to make quilt top.*

1. Sew 1 red **wide strip** and 1 light blue tonal **wide strip** together to make **Strip Set A**. Press seam allowances to red strip. Make 2 Strip Set A's. Cut across Strip Set A's at 2" intervals to make 40 **Unit 1's**.

Strip Set A
(make 2)

Unit 1
(make 40)

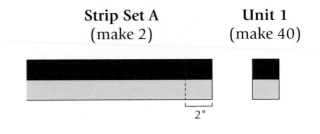

2. Sew 1 light blue tonal **wide strip** and 1 cream **wide strip** together to make **Strip Set B**. Press seam allowances to cream strip. Make 2 Strip Set B's. Cut across Strip Set B's at 2" intervals to make 40 **Unit 2's**.

Strip Set B
(make 2)

Unit 2
(make 40)

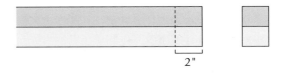

3. Sew 1 **Unit 1** and 1 **Unit 2** together to make **Unit 3**. Unit 3 should measure $3^1/_2$" x $3^1/_2$" including seam allowances. Make 40 Unit 3's.

Unit 3 (make 40)

4. Sew 1 **Unit 3** and 1 light blue tonal **small square** together to make **Unit 4**. Make 24 **Unit 4a's** and 16 **Unit 4b's**.

**Unit 4a**
(make 24)

**Unit 4b**
(make 16)

5. Sew 2 **Unit 4a's** together to make **Corner Block**. Block should measure $6^1/2$" x $6^1/2$" including seam allowances. Make 4 Corner Blocks.

**Corner Block** (make 4)

6. Sew 1 **Unit 4a** and 1 **Unit 4b** together to make **Chain Block**. Block should measure $6^1/2$" x $6^1/2$" including seam allowances. Make 16 Chain Blocks.

**Chain Block** (make 16)

## Making the Waves Blocks

1. Sew 1 medium blue tonal **narrow strip** and 1 light blue tonal **narrow strip** together to make **Strip Set C**. Press seam allowances to medium blue strip. Make 3 Strip Set C's. Cut across Strip Set C's at $1^9/16$" intervals to make 64 **Unit 5's**.

**Strip Set C**
(make 3)

**Unit 5**
(make 64)

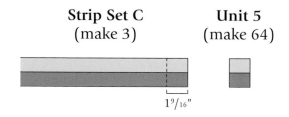

$1^9/16$"

2. Sew 2 **Unit 5's** together to make **Unit 6**. Unit 6 should measure $2^5/8$" x $2^5/8$" including seam allowances. Make 32 Unit 6's.

**Unit 6** (make 32)

3. Centering long edge of triangles, sew 2 medium blue tonal **small triangles** to opposite edges of 1 **Unit 6** as shown in **Fig. 1**. Sew 2 light blue tonal **small triangles** to remaining edges to make **Unit 7**. Trim Unit 7 to $3^1/2$" x $3^1/2$". Make 32 Unit 7's.

**Fig. 1**

**Unit 7** (make 32)

4. In the same manner, sew 2 medium blue tonal **medium triangles** and then 2 light blue tonal **medium triangles** to 1 **Unit 7** to make **Unit 8**. Trim Unit 8 to 4³/₄" x 4³/₄". Make 32 Unit 8's.

### Unit 8 (make 32)

5. In the same manner, sew 2 medium blue tonal **large triangles** and then 2 light blue tonal **large triangles** to 1 **Unit 8** to make **Waves Block**. Trim Block to 6¹/₂" x 6¹/₂". Make 32 Waves Block.

### Waves Blocks (make 32)

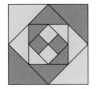

## Making the Center Panel

*Pay special attention to how each Chain Block is turned.*

1. Sew 2 **Chain Blocks** and 2 light blue tonal **medium squares** together to make **Unit 9**. Make 2 Unit 9's.

### Unit 9 (make 2)

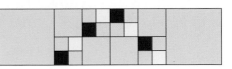

2. Sew 2 **Chain Blocks** together to make **Unit 10**. Make 2 Unit 10's.

### Unit 10 (make 2)

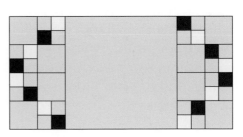

3. Sew 2 **Unit 10's** and blue tonal **center square** together to make **Unit 11**.

### Unit 11

69

4. Referring to **Center Panel** diagram, sew 2 **Unit 9's** and **Unit 11** together to make **pieced background**. Pieced background should measure 24¹/₂" x 24¹/₂" including seam allowances.

5. Working in alphabetical order, arrange appliqués **A-N** on **pieced background**; fuse in place. Using 2 strands of embroidery floss, Blanket Stitch (page 94) around all exposed edges of appliqués to make **Center Panel.**

### Center Panel

## Making the Compass Blocks

1. Center and fuse 1 of *each* appliqué **O-Q** on 1 light blue tonal **large square**. Using 2 strands of embroidery floss, Blanket Stitch appliqués to make **Compass Block**. Centering design, trim Block to 6¹/₂" x 6¹/₂". Make 4 Compass Blocks.

### Compass Block (make 4)

## Assembling the Quilt Top Center

*Pay special attention to how each block is turned.*

1. Sew 2 **Corner Blocks**, 4 **Waves Blocks**, and 2 light blue tonal **medium squares** together to make **Row A**. Make 2 Row A's.

### Row A (make 2)

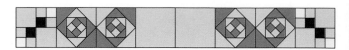

2. Sew 2 **Waves Blocks**, 2 **Compass Blocks**, 2 **Chain Blocks**, and 2 light blue tonal **medium squares** together to make **Row B**. Make 2 Row B's.

### Row B (make 2)

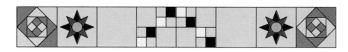

3. Sew 6 **Waves Blocks**, and 2 light blue tonal **medium squares** together to make **Row C**. Make 2 Row C's.

### Row C (make 2)

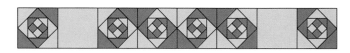

4. Sew 2 light blue tonal **medium squares** and 2 **Chain Blocks** together to make **Unit 12**. Make 2 Unit 12's.

**Unit 12** (make 2)

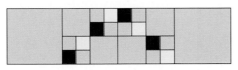

5. Sew 4 **Waves Blocks** together to make **Unit 13**. Make 2 Unit 13's.

**Unit 13** (make 2)

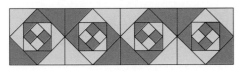

6. Sew 1 **Unit 12** and 1 **Unit 13** together to make **Unit 14**. Make 2 Unit 14's.

**Unit 14** (make 2)

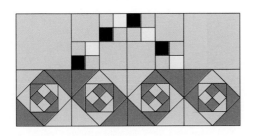

7. Sew 2 **Unit 14's** and **Center Panel** together to make **Row D**.

**Row D**

8. Referring to **Quilt Top Diagram**, page 73, sew **Rows** together to make quilt top center.

## Adding the Borders

1. Sew **inner border strips** together, end to end, to make one continuous strip.

2. Measure *length* across center of quilt top center. From continuous strip, cut 2 **side inner borders** the determined length. Matching centers and corners, sew side inner borders to quilt top center. Press seam allowances outward.

3. Measure *width* across center of quilt top center (including added borders). Cut 2 **top/bottom inner borders** the determined length. Matching centers and corners, sew top/bottom inner borders to quilt top center. Press seam allowances outward.

4. In the same manner and using **middle border strips** and **outer border strips**, add **middle** and **outer borders**. Press seam allowances outward.

## Completing the Quilt

1. Follow **Quilting**, page 89, to mark, layer, and quilt as desired. Quilt shown is machine quilted. The outer edges of the blocks and appliqués are quilted in the ditch. The light blue areas around the appliqués are stipple quilted. A feather is quilted in each light blue medium square. The Waves Blocks are quilted with overlapping circles and half-circles and the Corner and Chain Blocks are quilted with diagonal lines. The borders are cross-hatched quilted. (See photo of back of quilt.)

2. Follow **Making a Hanging Sleeve**, page 92, if a hanging sleeve is desired.

3. Use **binding strips** and follow **Binding**, page 92, to bind quilt.

**Back of Quilt**

## Quilt Top Diagram

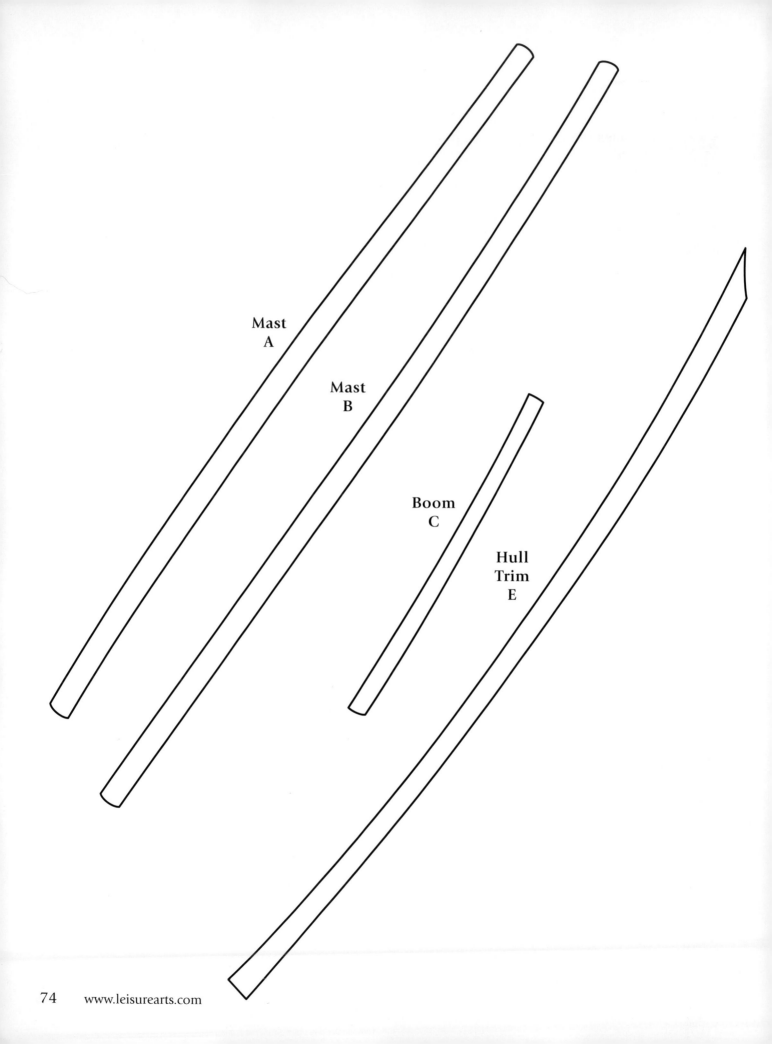

Mast
A

Mast
B

Boom
C

Hull
Trim
E

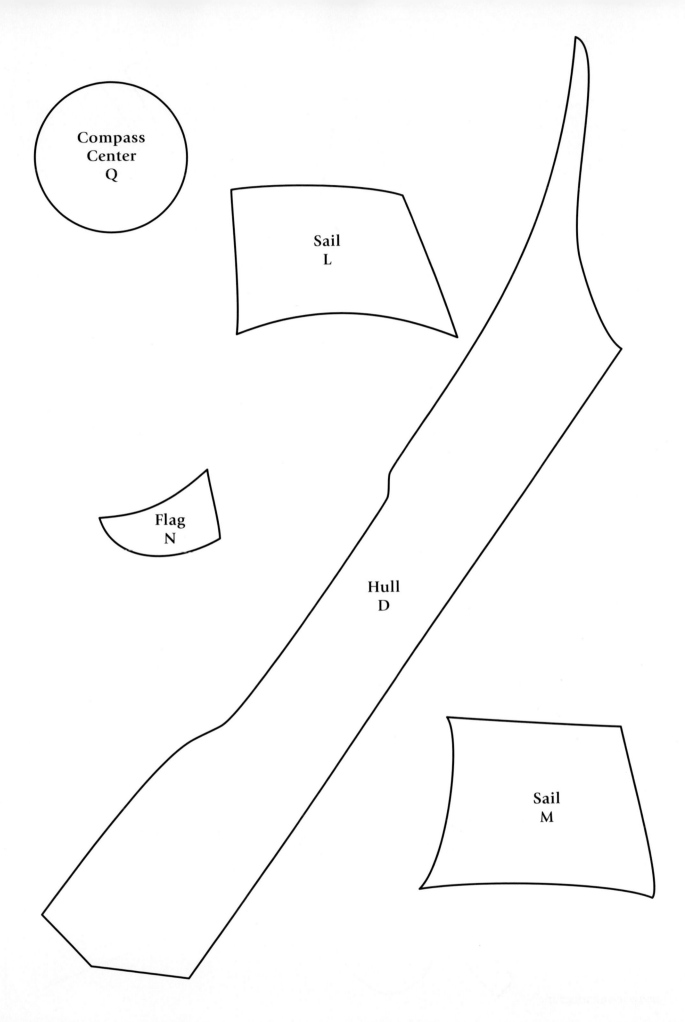

Compass
Center
Q

Sail
L

Flag
N

Hull
D

Sail
M

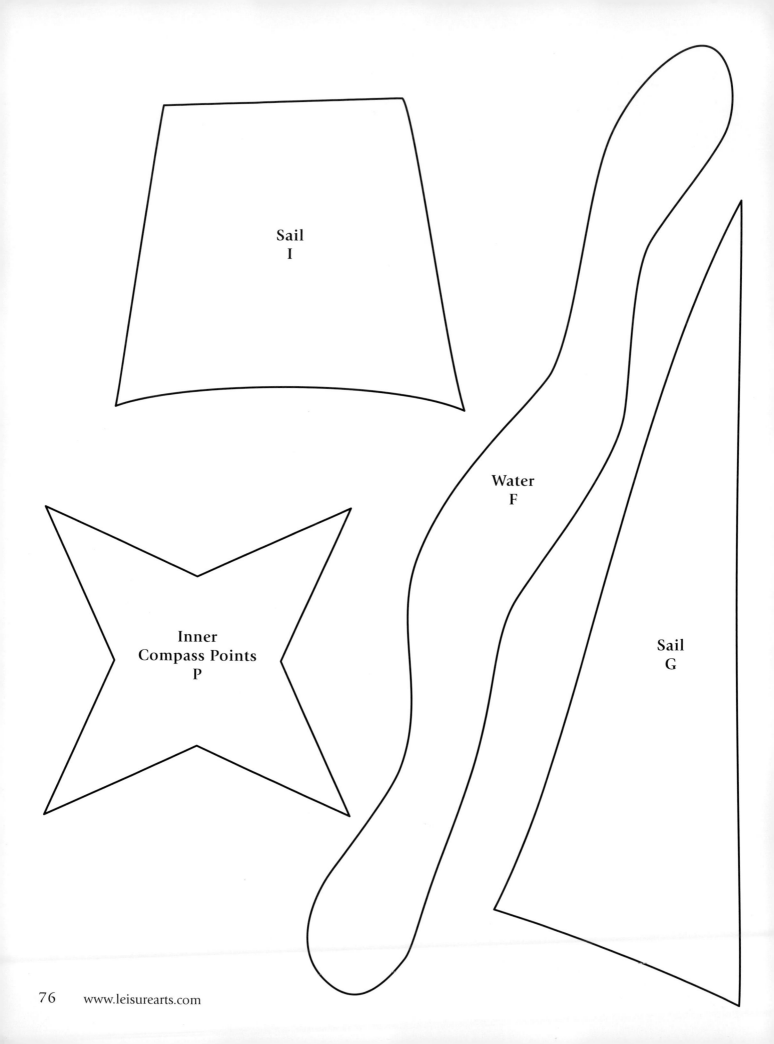

Sail
I

Inner
Compass Points
P

Water
F

Sail
G

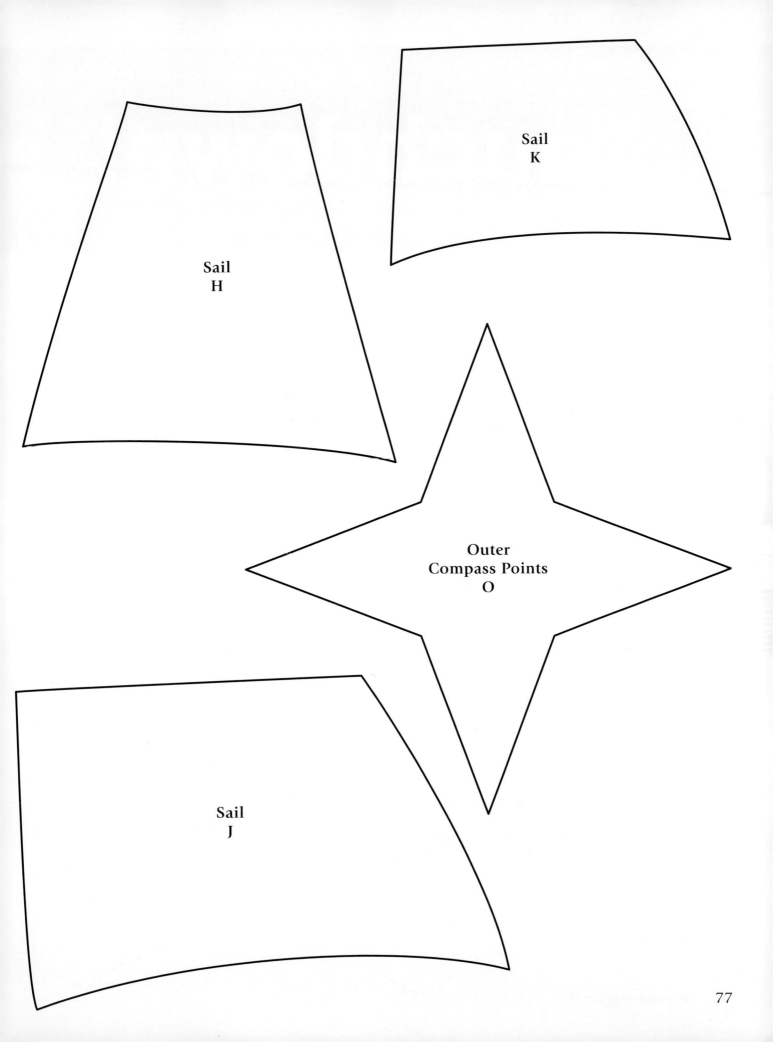

Sail
K

Sail
H

Outer
Compass Points
O

Sail
J

# Touchdown!

*Quilted by Doreen Clink.*

**Finished Quilt Size:** 60$\frac{1}{2}$" x 76$\frac{1}{2}$"
  (154 cm x 194 cm)
**Finished Block Size:** 8" x 8" (20 cm x 20 cm)

## Fabric Requirements

*Yardage is based on 43"/44" (109 cm/112 cm) wide fabric.*

2$\frac{3}{8}$ yds (2.2 m) of green batik
1$\frac{3}{8}$ yds (1.3 m) of brown batik
$\frac{3}{4}$ yd (69 cm) of rust batik
1$\frac{5}{8}$ yds (1.5 m) of cream print
$\frac{1}{2}$ yd (46 cm) of brown tonal
4$\frac{3}{4}$ yds (4.3 m) of fabric for backing
$\frac{1}{2}$ yd (46 cm) of fabric for binding

*You will also need:*

69" x 85" (175 cm x 216 cm) piece of batting
Paper-backed fusible web
Embroidery floss to match appliqués (cream
  print and brown tonal)

## Cutting the Pieces

*Follow **Rotary Cutting**, page 86, to cut fabric. Cut all strips from the selvage-to-selvage width. Center square and very large squares are cut larger than needed and will be trimmed after adding appliqués. All measurements include $\frac{1}{4}$" seam allowances.*

**From green batik:**

- Cut 7 **middle border strips** 2" wide.
- Cut 7 **strips** 2$\frac{1}{2}$" wide.
- Cut 1 **center square** 18$\frac{1}{2}$" x 18$\frac{1}{2}$".

*From remainder of width,*

- Cut 2 **very large squares** 10$\frac{1}{2}$" x 10$\frac{1}{2}$".

- Cut 2 strips 10$\frac{1}{2}$" wide. From these strips, cut 6 additional **very large squares** 10$\frac{1}{2}$" x 10$\frac{1}{2}$".
- Cut 1 strip 3$\frac{3}{8}$" wide. From this strip, cut 8 **small squares** 3$\frac{3}{8}$" x 3$\frac{3}{8}$".

**From brown batik:**

- Cut 7 **outer border strips** 3$\frac{1}{2}$" wide.
- Cut 4 strips 5" wide. From these strips, cut 28 **medium squares** 5" x 5".

**From rust batik:**

- Cut 7 **strips** 2$\frac{1}{2}$" wide.
- Cut 1 strip 3$\frac{3}{8}$" wide. From this strip, cut 8 **small squares** 3$\frac{3}{8}$" x 3$\frac{3}{8}$".

**From cream print:**

- Cut 6 **inner border strips** 2" wide.
- Cut 1 strip 8$\frac{1}{2}$" wide. From this strip, cut 4 **large squares** 8$\frac{1}{2}$" x 8$\frac{1}{2}$".
- Cut 4 strips 5" wide. From these strips, cut 28 **medium squares** 5" x 5".
- Cut 1 strip 3$\frac{3}{8}$" wide. From this strip, cut 4 **small squares** 3$\frac{3}{8}$" x 3$\frac{3}{8}$".

*From remainder of strip,*

- Cut 8 squares 3" x 3". Cut squares *once* diagonally to make 16 **small triangles**.
- Cut 1 strip 5$\frac{3}{8}$" wide. From this strip, cut 4 squares 5$\frac{3}{8}$" x 5$\frac{3}{8}$". Cut squares *twice* diagonally to make 16 **large triangles**.

**From fabric for binding:**

- Cut 8 **binding strips** 2" wide.

## Cutting the Appliqués

*Follow **Preparing Fusible Appliqués**, page 88, and use patterns, page 85, to cut appliqués.*

From brown tonal:

- Cut 12 **footballs**.

From cream print:

- Cut 12 sets of 2 **football trims**.
- Cut 12 **football laces**.

## Making the Football Blocks and Center Panel

1. Arrange 1 **football**, 1 set of **trims**, and 1 **football lace** in center of 1 green **very large square**; fuse in place. Using 2 strands of matching embroidery floss, Blanket Stitch (page 94) around all exposed edges of appliqués to make **Football Block**. Centering football, trim Block to $8^1/_2$" x $8^1/_2$". Make 8 Football Blocks.

**Football Block** (make 8)

2. Leaving approximately 2" around edges of square, arrange 4 **footballs**, 4 sets of **football trims**, and 4 **football laces** in center of green **center square**; fuse in place. In the same manner as before, Blanket Stitch appliqués to make **Football Center Panel**. Centering design, trim Football Center Panel to $16^1/_2$" x $16^1/_2$".

**Football Center Panel**

## Making the Diamond Blocks

*Follow **Piecing**, page 87, and **Pressing**, page 88, to make quilt top.*

1. Aligning right angle of each triangle with corner of square, sew 2 cream **large triangles** and 1 green **small square** together to make **Unit 1**. Make 8 Unit 1's.

**Unit 1** (make 8)

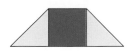

2. Centering long edge of triangle, sew 1 **small triangle** and 1 **Unit 1** together to make **Unit 2**. Make 8 Unit 2's.

**Unit 2** (make 8)

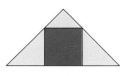

3. Sew 2 rust **small squares** and 1 cream **small square** together to make **Unit 3**. Make 4 Unit 3's.

**Unit 3** (make 4)

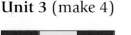

4. Centering long edge of each triangle, sew 2 **small triangles** and 1 **Unit 3** together to make **Unit 4**. Make 4 Unit 4's.

**Unit 4** (make 4)

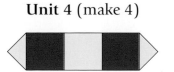

5. Sew 2 **Unit 2's** and 1 **Unit 4** together to make **Diamond Block**. Trim Block to $8^1/2$" x $8^1/2$". Make 4 Diamond Blocks.

**Diamond Block** (make 4)

## Making the Chain Blocks

1. Sew 1 green **strip** and 1 rust **strip** together to make **Strip Set**. Make 7 Strip Sets. Cut across Strip Sets at $2^1/2$" intervals to make 112 **Unit 5's**.

**Strip Set**
(make 7)

**Unit 5**
(make 112)

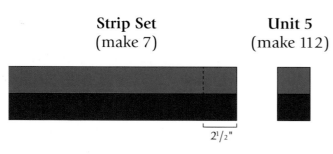

$2^1/2$"

2. Sew 2 **Unit 5's** together to make **Unit 6**. Make 56 Unit 6's.

**Unit 6** (make 56)

3. Draw a diagonal line on wrong side of each cream **medium square**.

4. Matching right sides, place 1 cream **medium square** on top of 1 brown **medium square**. Stitch $1/4$" from each side of drawn line (**Fig. 1**). Cut along drawn line and press seam allowances to darker fabric to make 2 **Triangle-Squares**. Trim each Triangle-Square to $4^1/2$" x $4^1/2$". Make 56 Triangle-Squares.

**Fig. 1**

**Triangle-Square** (make 56)

5. Sew 1 **Triangle-Square** and 1 **Unit 6** together to make **Unit 7**. Make 56 Unit 7's.

**Unit 7** (make 56)

6. Sew 2 **Unit 7's** together to make **Chain Block**. Make 28 Chain Blocks.

**Chain Block** (make 28)

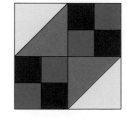

## Assembling the Quilt Top Center

1. Sew 4 **Football Blocks** and 2 **Diamond Blocks** together to make **Row A**. Make 2 Row A's.

**Row A** (make 2)

2. Sew 6 **Chain Blocks** together to make **Row B**. Make 2 Row B's.

**Row B** (make 2)

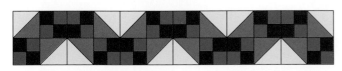

3. Sew 4 **Chain Blocks** and 2 cream **large squares** together to make **Row C**. Make 2 Row C's.

**Row C** (make 2)

4. Sew 4 **Chain Blocks** together to make **Unit 8**. Make 2 Unit 8's.

**Unit 8** (make 2)

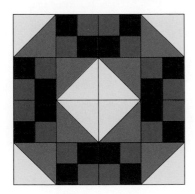

5. Sew 2 **Unit 8's** and **Football Center Panel** together to make **Row D**.

**Row D**

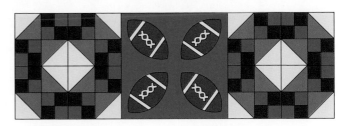

6. Referring to **Quilt Top Diagram**, page 84, sew **Rows** together to make quilt top center.

## Adding the Borders

1. Sew **inner border strips** together, end to end, to make one continuous strip.
2. Measure *length* across center of quilt top center. From continuous strip, cut 2 **side inner borders** the determined length. Matching centers and corners, sew side inner borders to quilt top center. Press seam allowances outward.
3. Measure *width* across center of quilt top center (including added borders). Cut 2 **top/bottom inner borders** the determined length. Matching centers and corners, sew top/bottom inner borders to quilt top center. Press seam allowances outward.
4. In the same manner and using **middle border strips** and **outer border strips**, add **middle** and **outer borders**. Press seam allowances outward.

## Completing the Quilt

1. Follow **Quilting**, page 89, to mark, layer, and quilt as desired. Quilt shown is machine quilted. The appliqués are quilted in the ditch. The remainder of the quilt is quilted with an all-over pattern which includes footballs and goal posts. (See photo of back of quilt, page 85.)
2. Follow **Making a Hanging Sleeve**, page 92, if a hanging sleeve is desired.
3. Use **binding strips** and follow **Binding**, page 92, to bind quilt.

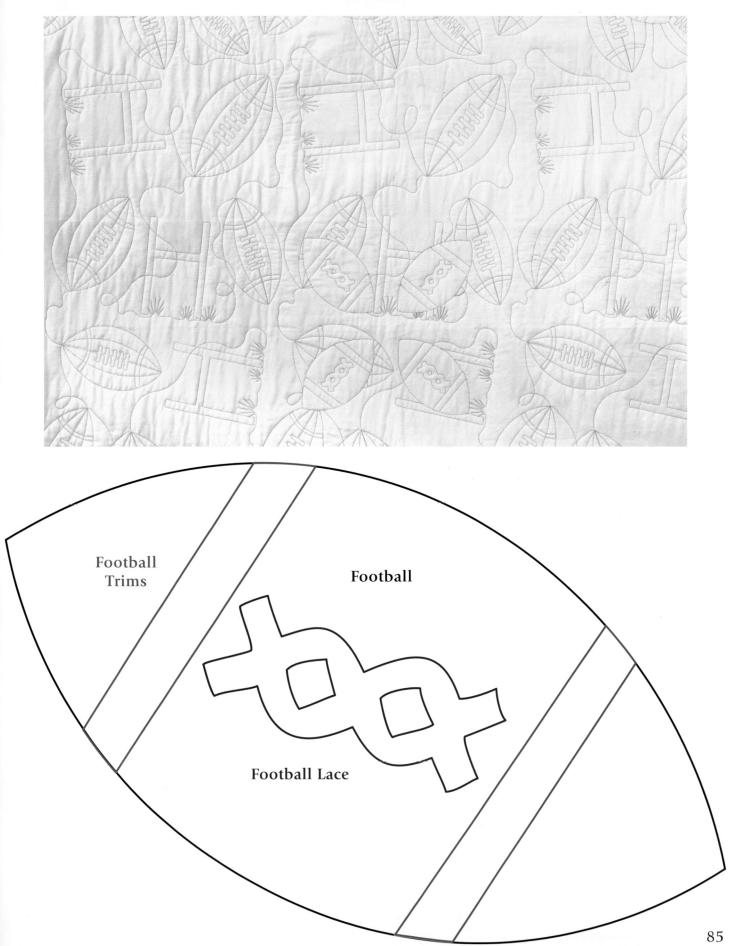

Football
Trims

Football

Football Lace

# General Instructions

*To make your quilting easier and more enjoyable, we encourage you to carefully read all of the general instructions, study the color photographs, and familiarize yourself with the individual project instructions before beginning a project.*

## Fabrics

### SELECTING FABRICS

Choose high-quality, medium-weight 100% cotton fabrics. All-cotton fabrics hold a crease better, fray less, and are easier to quilt than cotton/polyester blends.

Yardage requirements listed for each project are based on 43"/44" wide fabric with a "usable" width of 40" after shrinkage and trimming selvages. Actual usable width will probably vary slightly from fabric to fabric. Our recommended yardage lengths should be adequate for occasional re-squaring of fabric when many cuts are required.

### PREPARING FABRICS

Pre-washing fabrics may cause edges to ravel. As a result, your fat quarters or other pre-cut pieces may not be large enough to cut all of the pieces required for your chosen project. Therefore, we do not recommend pre-washing your yardage or pre-cut fabrics. (Refer to **Caring for Your Quilt**, page 95, for instructions on washing your finished quilt.)

Before cutting, prepare fabrics with a steam iron set on cotton and starch or sizing. The starch or sizing will give the fabric a crisp finish. This will make cutting more accurate and may make piecing easier.

## Rotary Cutting

### CUTTING FROM YARDAGE

- Place fabric yardage on work surface with fold closest to you.

- Cut all strips from the selvage-to-selvage width of the fabric unless otherwise indicated in project instructions.

- Square left edge of fabric using rotary cutter and rulers (**Figs. 1-2**).

**Fig. 1**

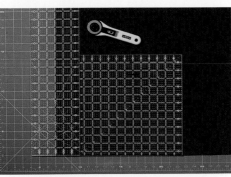

**Fig. 2**

- To cut each strip required for a project, place ruler over cut edge of fabric, aligning desired marking on ruler with cut edge; make cut (**Fig. 3**).

**Fig. 3**

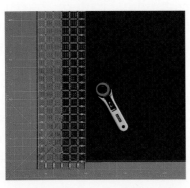

- When cutting several strips from a single piece of fabric, it is important to make sure that cuts remain at a perfect right angle to the fold; square fabric as needed.

## CUTTING FROM FAT QUARTERS

- Place fabric flat on work surface with lengthwise (18") edge closest to you.

- Cut all strips parallel to 21" edge of the fabric unless otherwise indicated in project instructions.

- To cut each strip required for a project, place ruler over left edge of fabric, aligning desired marking on ruler with left edge; make cut.

# Piecing

*Precise cutting, followed by accurate piecing, will ensure that all pieces of quilt top fit together well.*

- Set sewing machine stitch length for approximately 11 stitches per inch.

- Use neutral-colored general-purpose sewing thread (not quilting thread) in needle and in bobbin.

- A consistent seam allowance is *essential*. Presser feet that are $1/4$" wide are available for most sewing machines.

- When piecing, always place pieces right sides together and match raw edges; pin if necessary.

- Chain piecing saves time and will usually result in more accurate piecing.

- Trim away points of seam allowances that extend beyond edges of sewn pieces.

## SEWING STRIP SETS

When there are several strips to assemble into a strip set, first sew strips together into pairs, then sew pairs together to form strip set. To help avoid distortion, sew seams in opposite directions (**Fig. 4**).

**Fig. 4**

## SEWING ACROSS SEAM INTERSECTIONS

When sewing across intersection of two seams, place pieces right sides together and match seams exactly, making sure seam allowances are pressed in opposite directions (**Fig. 5**).

**Fig. 5**

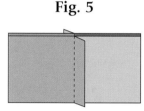

## SEWING SHARP POINTS

To ensure sharp points when joining triangular or diagonal pieces, stitch across the center of the "X" (shown in pink) formed on wrong side by previous seams (**Fig. 6**).

**Fig. 6**

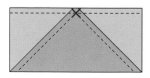

# Pressing

- Use steam iron set on "Cotton" for all pressing.

- Press after sewing each seam.

- Seam allowances are almost always pressed to one side, usually toward the darker fabric. However, to reduce bulk, it may be necessary to press seam allowances toward the lighter fabric or even to press them open.

- To prevent dark fabric seam allowance from showing through light fabric, trim darker seam allowance slightly narrower than lighter seam allowance.

- To press long seams, such as those in long strip sets, without curving or other distortion, lay strips across width of the ironing board.

## PREPARING FUSIBLE APPLIQUÉS

*Patterns for fused appliqués are printed in reverse to enable you to use the speedy method of preparing appliqués following the steps below. White or light-colored fabrics may need to be lined with fusible interfacing before applying fusible web to prevent darker fabrics from showing through.*

1. Place paper-backed fusible web, paper side up, over appliqué pattern. Trace pattern onto paper side of web with pencil as many times as indicated in project instructions for a single fabric.
2. If the instructions call for appliqué pieces "in reverse," it is because the shape will be facing both directions. Use a black fine-point marker to trace the pattern onto plain white paper. Flip the paper over and trace over drawn lines. Using this for your pattern, repeat Step 1.
3. Follow manufacturer's instructions to fuse traced patterns to wrong side of fabrics. Do not remove paper backing.
4. Use scissors to cut out appliqué pieces along traced lines. Remove paper backing from all pieces.

# Quilting

*Quilting holds the three layers (top, batting, and backing) of the quilt together. Because marking, layering, and quilting are interrelated and may be done in different orders depending on circumstances, please read entire **Quilting** section, pages 89-91, before beginning project.*

## TYPES OF QUILTING DESIGNS

### In the Ditch Quilting

Quilting along seamlines or along edges of appliquéd pieces is called "in the ditch" quilting. This type of quilting should be done on side **opposite** seam allowance and does not have to be marked.

### Outline Quilting

Quilting a consistent distance, usually $1/4$", from seam or appliqué edge is called "outline" quilting. Outline quilting may be marked, or $1/4$" wide masking tape may be placed along seamlines for quilting guide. (Do not leave tape on quilt longer than necessary, since it may leave an adhesive residue.)

### Motif Quilting

Quilting a design, such as a feathered wreath, is called "motif" quilting. This type of quilting should be marked before basting quilt layers together.

### Echo Quilting

Quilting that follows the outline of an appliquéd or pieced design with two or more parallel lines is called "echo" quilting. This type of quilting does not need to be marked.

### Channel Quilting

Quilting with straight, parallel lines is called "channel" quilting. This type of quilting may be marked or stitched using a guide.

### Crosshatch Quilting

Quilting straight lines in a grid pattern is called "crosshatch" quilting. Lines may be stitched parallel to edges of quilt or stitched diagonally. This type of quilting may be marked or stitched using a guide.

### Meandering Quilting

Quilting in random curved lines and swirls is called "meandering" quilting. Quilting lines should not cross or touch each other. This type of quilting does not need to be marked.

### Stipple Quilting

Meandering quilting that is very closely spaced is called "stipple" quilting. Stippling will flatten the area quilted and is often stitched in background areas to raise appliquéd or pieced designs. This type of quilting does not need to be marked.

## MARKING QUILTING LINES

Quilting lines may be marked using fabric marking pencils, chalk markers, or water- or air-soluble pens.

Simple quilting designs may be marked with chalk or chalk pencil after basting. A small area may be marked, then quilted, before moving to next area to be marked. Intricate designs should be marked before basting using a more durable marker.

*Caution:* Pressing may permanently set some marks. **Test** different markers **on scrap fabric** to find one that marks clearly and can be thoroughly removed.

A wide variety of pre-cut quilting stencils, as well as entire books of quilting patterns, are available. Using a stencil makes it easier to mark intricate or repetitive designs.

To make a stencil from a pattern, center template plastic over pattern and use a permanent marker to trace pattern onto plastic. Use a craft knife with single or double blade to cut channels along traced lines (**Fig. 7**).

**Fig. 7**

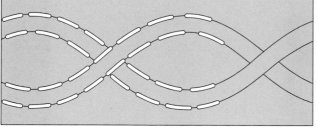

## PREPARING THE BACKING

*To allow for slight shifting of quilt top during quilting, backing should be approximately 4" larger on all sides. Yardage requirements listed for quilt backings are calculated for 43"/44" wide fabric. Using 90" wide or 108" wide fabric for the backing may eliminate piecing. To piece a backing using 43"/44" wide fabric, use the following instructions.*

1.  Measure length and width of quilt top; add 8" to each measurement.
2.  Cut backing fabric into two lengths the determined *length* measurement. Trim selvages. Place lengths with right sides facing and sew long edges together, forming a tube (**Fig. 8**). Match seams and press along one fold (**Fig. 9**). Cut along pressed fold to form a single piece (**Fig. 10**).

| Fig. 8 | Fig. 9 | Fig. 10 |

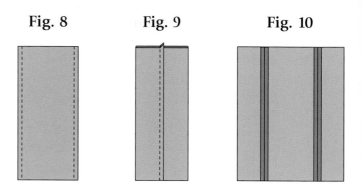

3.  Trim backing to size determined in Step 1; press seam allowances open.

## CHOOSING THE BATTING

The appropriate batting will make quilting easier. All cotton or cotton/polyester blend battings work well for machine quilting because the cotton helps "grip" quilt layers.

Types of batting include cotton, polyester, wool, cotton/polyester blend, cotton/wool blend, and silk.

When selecting batting, refer to package labels for characteristics and care instructions. Cut batting same size as prepared backing.

## ASSEMBLING THE QUILT

1. Examine wrong side of quilt top closely; trim any seam allowances and clip any threads that may show through front of the quilt. Press quilt top, being careful not to "set" any marked quilting lines.
2. Place backing *wrong* side up on flat surface. Use masking tape to tape edges of backing to surface. Place batting on top of backing fabric. Smooth batting gently, being careful not to stretch or tear. Center quilt top *right* side up on batting.
3. Use 1" rustproof safety pins to "pin-baste" all layers together, spacing pins approximately 4" apart. Begin at center and work toward outer edges to secure all layers. If possible, place pins away from areas that will be quilted, although pins may be removed as needed when quilting.

## QUILTING METHODS

Use general-purpose thread in bobbin. Do not use quilting thread. Thread the needle of machine with general-purpose thread or transparent monofilament thread to make quilting blend with quilt top fabrics. Use decorative thread, such as a metallic or contrasting-color general-purpose thread, to make quilting lines stand out more.

### Straight-Line Quilting

*The term "straight-line" is somewhat deceptive, since curves (especially gentle ones) as well as straight lines can be stitched with this technique.*

1. Set stitch length for six to ten stitches per inch and attach a walking foot to sewing machine.
2. Determine which section of quilt will have longest continuous quilting line, oftentimes the area from center top to center bottom. Roll up and secure each edge of quilt to help reduce the bulk, keeping fabrics smooth.
3. Begin stitching on longest quilting line, using very short stitches for the first $1/4$" to "lock" quilting. Stitch across project, using one hand on each side of walking foot to slightly spread fabric and to guide fabric through machine. Lock stitches at end of quilting line.
4. Continue machine quilting, stitching longer quilting lines first to stabilize quilt before moving on to other areas.

### Free-Motion Quilting

*Free-motion quilting may be free form or may follow a marked pattern.*

1. Attach darning foot to sewing machine and lower or cover feed dogs.
2. Position quilt under darning foot; lower foot. Holding top thread, take a stitch and pull bobbin thread to top of quilt. To "lock" beginning of quilting line, hold top and bobbin threads while making three to five stitches in place.
3. Use one hand on each side of darning foot to slightly spread fabric and to move fabric through the machine. Even stitch length is achieved by using smooth, flowing hand motion and steady machine speed. Slow machine speed and fast hand movement will create long stitches. Fast machine speed and slow hand movement will create short stitches. Move quilt sideways, back and forth, in a circular motion, or in a random motion to create desired designs; do not rotate quilt. Lock stitches at end of each quilting line.

# Making a Hanging Sleeve

*Attaching a hanging sleeve to the back of a quilt before the binding is added will allow you to display the quilt on a wall.*

1. Measure width of quilt top edge and subtract 1". Cut piece of fabric 7" wide by determined measurement.
2. Press short edges of fabric piece ¼" to wrong side; press edges ¼" to wrong side again and machine stitch in place.
3. Matching wrong sides, fold piece in half lengthwise to form tube.
4. Follow project instructions to sew binding to quilt top and to trim backing and batting. Before Blindstitching binding to backing, match raw edges and stitch hanging sleeve to center top edge on back of quilt.
5. Finish binding quilt, treating hanging sleeve as part of backing.
6. Blindstitch bottom of hanging sleeve to backing, taking care not to stitch through to front of quilt.
7. Insert dowel or slat into hanging sleeve.

# Binding

1. Using a diagonal seam (**Fig. 11**), sew binding strips called for in project together end to end.

**Fig. 11**

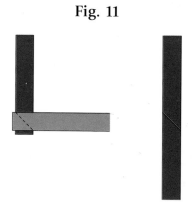

2. Matching wrong sides and raw edges, press strips in half lengthwise to complete binding.
3. Beginning with one end near center on bottom edge of quilt, lay binding around quilt to make sure that seams in binding will not end up at a corner. Adjust placement if necessary. Matching raw edges of binding to raw edge of quilt top, pin binding to right side of quilt along one edge.
4. When you reach first corner, mark ¼" from corner of quilt top (**Fig. 12**).

**Fig. 12**

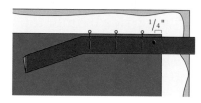

5. Beginning approximately 10" from end of binding and using ¼" seam allowance, sew binding to quilt, backstitching at beginning of stitching and at mark (**Fig. 13**). Lift needle out of fabric and clip thread.

**Fig. 13**

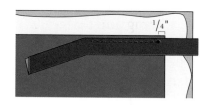

6. Fold binding as shown in **Figs. 14-15** and pin binding to adjacent side, matching raw edges. When you've reached the next corner, mark ¼" from edge of quilt top.

**Fig. 14**          **Fig. 15**

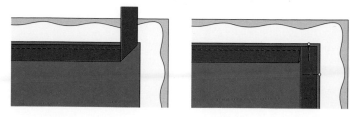

7. Backstitching at edge of quilt top, sew pinned binding to quilt (**Fig. 16**); backstitch at the next mark. Lift needle out of fabric and clip thread.

**Fig. 16**

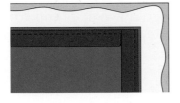

8. Continue sewing binding to quilt, stopping approximately 10" from starting point (**Fig. 17**).

**Fig. 17**

9. Bring beginning and end of binding to center of opening and fold each end back, leaving a ¹/₄" space between folds (**Fig. 18**). Finger press folds.

**Fig. 18**

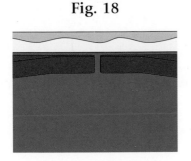

10. Unfold ends of binding and draw a line across wrong side in finger-pressed crease. Draw a line through the lengthwise pressed fold of binding at the same spot to create a cross mark. With edge of ruler at cross mark, line up 45° angle marking on ruler with one long side of binding. Draw a diagonal line from edge to edge. Repeat on remaining end, making sure that the two diagonal lines are angled the same way (**Fig. 19**).

**Fig. 19**

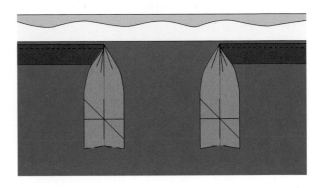

11. Matching right sides and diagonal lines, pin binding ends together at right angles (**Fig. 20**).

**Fig. 20**

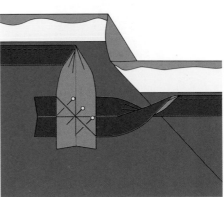

12. Machine stitch along diagonal line (**Fig. 21**), removing pins as you stitch.

**Fig. 21**

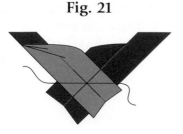

13. Lay binding against quilt to double check that it is correct length.
14. Trim binding ends, leaving ¹/₄" seam allowances; press seam open. Stitch binding to quilt.
15. Trim backing and batting even with quilt top.
16. On one edge of quilt, fold binding over to quilt backing and pin pressed edge in place, covering stitching line (**Fig. 22**). On adjacent side, fold binding over, forming a mitered corner (**Fig. 23**). Repeat to pin remainder of binding in place.

**Fig. 22**

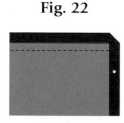

**Fig. 23**

17. Blindstitch (**Fig. 24**) binding to backing, taking care not to stitch through to front of quilt.

# Hand Stitches

## BLIND STITCH

Come up at 1, go down at 2, and come up at 3 (**Fig. 24**). Repeat steps 2 and 3 to continue working. Length of stitches may be varied as desired.

**Fig. 24**

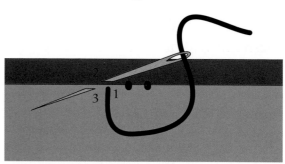

## BLANKET STITCH

Come up at 1. Holding thread below needle, go down at 2 and come up at 3 (**Fig. 25**). Repeat steps 2 and 3 to continue working.

**Fig. 25**

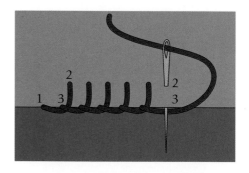

## COUCHING

Anchor thread #1 at one end. Using thread #2 to sew thread #1 in place, come up at 1 and go down at 2 (**Fig. 26**).

**Fig. 26**

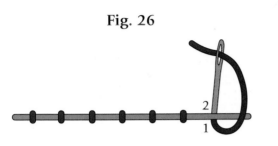

# Caring for Your Quilt

- Wash finished quilt in cold water on gentle cycle with mild soap. Soaps which have no softeners, fragrances, whiteners, or other additives are safest. Rinse twice in cold water.

- Use a dye magnet, such as Shout® Color Catcher®, each time quilt is washed to absorb any dyes that bleed. When washing quilt the first time, you may choose to use two color catchers for extra caution.

- Dry quilt on low heat/air fluff in 15 minute increments until dry.

# Signing and Dating Your Quilt

*A completed quilt is a work of art and should be signed and dated. There are many different ways to do this and numerous books on the subject. The label should reflect the style of the quilt, the occasion or person for which it was made, and the quilter's own particular talents. The following are suggestions for recording the history of the quilt or adding a sentiment for future generations.*

- Embroider quilter's name, date, and any additional information on quilt top or backing. Matching floss, such as cream floss on white border, will leave a subtle record. Bright or contrasting floss will make the information stand out.

- Make label from muslin and use permanent marker to write information. Use different colored permanent markers to make label more decorative. Stitch label to back of quilt.

- Use photo-transfer paper to add image to white or cream fabric label. Stitch label to back of quilt.

- Piece an extra block from quilt top pattern to use as label. Add information with permanent fabric pen. Appliqué block to back of quilt.

- Write a message on an appliquéd design from the quilt top. Attach appliqué to back of quilt.

## Metric Conversion Chart

| | |
|---|---|
| Inches x 2.54 = centimeters (cm) | Yards x .9144 = meters (m) |
| Inches x 25.4 = millimeters (mm) | Yards x 91.44 = centimeters (cm) |
| Inches x .0254 = meters (m) | Centimeters x .3937 = inches (") |
| | Meters x 1.0936 = yards (yd) |

### Standard Equivalents

| | | | | | |
|---|---|---|---|---|---|
| $1/8$" | 3.2 mm | 0.32 cm | $1/8$ yard | 11.43 cm | 0.11 m |
| $1/4$" | 6.35 mm | 0.635 cm | $1/4$ yard | 22.86 cm | 0.23 m |
| $3/8$" | 9.5 mm | 0.95 cm | $3/8$ yard | 34.29 cm | 0.34 m |
| $1/2$" | 12.7 mm | 1.27 cm | $1/2$ yard | 45.72 cm | 0.46 m |
| $5/8$" | 15.9 mm | 1.59 cm | $5/8$ yard | 57.15 cm | 0.57 m |
| $3/4$" | 19.1 mm | 1.91 cm | $3/4$ yard | 68.58 cm | 0.69 m |
| $7/8$" | 22.2 mm | 2.22 cm | $7/8$ yard | 80 cm | 0.8 m |
| 1" | 25.4 mm | 2.54 cm | 1 yard | 91.44 cm | 0.91 m |

Notes: _____

_____

_____

_____

_____

_____

_____

_____

_____

_____

_____

_____

_____

_____

_____

_____

_____

_____

_____

_____

_____

_____